Cambridge Computer Science Texts · 5

An Introduction to the Uses of Computers

MURRAY LAVER

Cambridge University Press

CAMBRIDGE

LONDON · NEW YORK · MELBOURNE

Published by the Syndics of the Cambridge University Press

The Pitt Building, Trumpington Street, Cambridge CB2 1RP

Bentley House, 200 Euston Road, London NW1 2DB

32 East 57th Street, New York, NY 10022, USA

296 Beaconsfield Parade, Middle Park, Melbourne 3206, Australia

First published 1976

Printed in Great Britain

at the University Printing House, Cambridge

(Euan Phillips, University Printer)

Library of Congress Cataloging in Publication Data

Laver, F.J.M.
    An introduction to the uses of computers.

    (Cambridge computer science texts ; 5)
    Includes bibliographies and index.
    1. Electronic data processing. 2. Electronic
digital computers. I. Title.
QA76.L33   001.6'4   75-23535

ISBN 0 521 29035 X

A z
L

Contents

Preface

Computers are here to stay, and it is important that as many men and women as possible should acquire an easy familiarity with them in the ordinary course of their education. In that way they will be spared those fears that derive from grossly inflated ideas about the powers or the autonomy of 'electronic brains', and they will have no need to affect that fastidious disdain for mere machinery with which some now seek to conceal their ignorance of computation.

This introductory book is intended for those who are not specializing in computer science but need to know enough about computers and their uses to understand how they are, or could be, applied to the subjects of special interest to them. For this purpose it is essential to appreciate that computers are very much more than high-speed arithmetic machines; and how it is they can handle information of many different kinds, and by a range of processes much wider than the purely mathematical. The book therefore illustrates a number of its topics by examples drawn from commercial data processing - not least because this lies outside the direct experience of most full-time students.

The book is aimed, also, at those who are learning to use some particular programming language: to them, it offers a background of general information about computers and their uses, and an introduction to the meanings of the extensive and confusing terminology of computing. The book will accordingly be appropriate for many taking courses in computing in universities and colleges, or who are studying independently. For these last, notes are provided on the solutions to the example which are included at the end of each chapter to allow the student to test his understanding of the material presented.

The use of computers is permeating every aspect of our lives and this, with their rapidly increasing use of telecommunication channels for the automatic exchange of data, is bound to exert a significant influence on the organization and conduct of most of our activities. There could be some disturbing consequences unless we watch, direct and prune the lush growth of computer systems; and the book attempts to give a non-specialist reader enough understanding of the character, power and limitations of computers to be able to play an informed layman's part in guiding their application. Only thus can we hope to use them without too much risk of unpleasant side effects.

F.J.M.L.

Sidmouth, Devon
Summer 1975

1· Function and form

1.1 *Myth and reality*

No one can doubt that computers have acquired a somewhat tarnished public image. They are frequently presented as mechanical tyrants which threaten our jobs and our liberty, and which are expelling the last vestiges of personal service from shopping, banking, medicine and education. 'Computer predicts' is a common start to headlines that end unpleasantly. However, computers are no more than tools; it is we who decide what to use them for, and what methods to employ: no law of nature, man or economics dictates what they shall do, and no impersonal technological imperative drives their development in directions, or at speeds, that we are powerless to prevent. This is all obvious enough; why is it not accepted as fact? Two reasons can be suggested.

First, there is a widespread belief that computers are inscrutable instruments which operate in mysterious ways that lie far beyond even the possibility of comprehension by ordinary men and women: and what we do not understand, we fear; and what we fear, we hate. This belief is false for, as we shall see, the operating principles of computers are essentially simple. It is not necessary to be a mathematician or an electronic engineer to learn enough about how computers work, and how they are put to work, to be able to use them effectively, and to discuss how they might affect the ways in which we live.

Second, while we have come to feel at home with machine tools that extend and enlarge our muscle power we feel uneasy when faced by machines that offer to do the same for our mental capacity. We regard rational thinking as one of the distinguishing marks of mankind, and it disturbs us to find a machine apparently operating in the same area; nor are our qualms lessened when we note that the same computer can be used for purposes so varied as scientific calculation, compiling an index, checking St. Paul's authorship of the Epistles, playing a modest game of chess, working out invoices and bills, setting up telephone directories for printing, and controlling the traffic lights of a small town. As we shall see, this variety does not derive from complexity in the construction of the machine, but from the fact that we have designed it to follow the paths *we* have charted through lengthy sequences of individually simple actions. As an analogy, the letters of the alphabet, also, are simple and few in number but can be combined into sequences that express whatever we care to write. In each case the power and the variety come from the creative skill of the men and women who form the elementary units, letters or computer instructions, into relevant and effective sequences.

Here is the essence of the invention; the key fact about computers is that they are controlled by reference to a list of *instructions* which sets out in complete detail and in order, tiny step by tiny step, exactly which operations are to be performed. This list we call the *program* for the job. Each job has to have its own computer program, but it is quick and easy to replace the program for one job with that for another when the first has been completed and the computer is ready for the second. Incidentally, the original English spelling is the accepted way to refer to a computer 'program', and it leaves the 19th century novelty 'programme' for everyday use.

The next few chapters show how control by programs allows us to apply computers to so wide a diversity of tasks; and what

2

kind of help they can give in that handling of information which supports so many of our activities. This will prepare the ground for a series of reviews of the applications of computers, and for some appraisals of the economic and social consequences that could flow from their increasing use. These introductory chapters cannot avoid some rather detailed accounts of computer construction, operation and programming, and they can be skipped by proceeding direct to chapter 7; but this course is not recommended to those who are new to the subject, for it would deny them the background information they will need when reading the later text with that well-founded scepticism which it is so necessary to bring to any discussion of social or economic affairs.

1.2 *Programmed control*

A computer and its programs resemble a gramophone and its records. Thus, a gramophone is a completely general-purpose musical instrument, but without a record it is silent; put on the corresponding record and it can sound like a symphony orchestra, a brass band, or a pop singer. A library of records provides a wide and expansible choice of music; and similarly, a library of computer programs allows us to perform a wide and expansible range of jobs. However, should we want to hear a specific item played by one particular orchestra we can do so quickly and easily only if that orchestra has already recorded that item. If not, then to make a record would involve rehearsal, recording and pressing – a lengthy and expensive business. Similarly with computers, when no program is already available for the job we may have to spend a great deal of time and money in preparing one. We return to this point in chapter 4.

As written, a typical computer instruction consists of two parts. First, there is the *function part* which may be a group of numerals but, more usually, is a string of letters that in-

dicates – often in a mnemonic code – what is to be done, for
example, ADD; and we might also have SUB, MUL, and DIV, all
with their obvious meanings. A large computer may have a repertoire of 100 or more different functions in its *instruction
set*, or *order code* as it is also called. Second, there is the
address part of the instruction which indicates where the quantity to be operated upon (the *operand*) is to be found; for example in the instruction ADD 3405, the operand is being held
in compartment number 3405 of the store, which is the part of
the computer used to hold the data taking part in the computation.

When it is actually controlling the computer the program,
also, is held in the store; and its instructions, and the data,
are each converted into groups of *binary digits*, invariably
abbreviated to *bits*. Thus, ADD 3405 might become: 00111010100-
1101. Binary representation is used because it is much easier
to design electronic equipment to discriminate reliably between
only two levels of electric current – on and off – than between
say, the ten different levels which would be needed to represent decimal numbers directly. The electrical signals used con-
sist of very brief pulses of current lasting less than a mill-
ionth of a second and following each other in a regular sequence
like the ticks of a clock: the presence of a pulse can stand
for binary 1, and the omission of a pulse when one is due can
stand for binary 0.

1.3 *Representation of data*
We need at this point to enter into a rather dry, but
brief, consideration of how data are represented inside a computer.[3]   The data comprise letters, numerals, punctuation
marks and other symbols which, for ease of reference, can be
lumped together and called *characters*. The usual practice is
to process this data in chunks which are known, rather confus-

4

ingly, as *words*. Different computers use chunks of different sizes, commonly in the range 8 to 64 bits. One computer word can be used to represent a binary number, or it may be divided into sections of 8 bits which are known as *bytes*. The eight bits of a byte can be arranged in $2^8 = 256$ different ways, and so we can use it to represent any of the characters in common use. For purely numerical data however, we need no more than four bits for a decimal digit ($2^4 = 16$), and the use of a separate group of four bits for each digit of a decimal number is termed *binary coded decimal,* or *BCD*. Clearly, each byte can hold two such digits, and 3405 might be represented, in what is called *packed decimal* form, by the two bytes: 0011, 0100; 0000, 0101. Alternatively, one byte can be used to represent two *hexadecimal* digits, that is digits in the scale of 16.

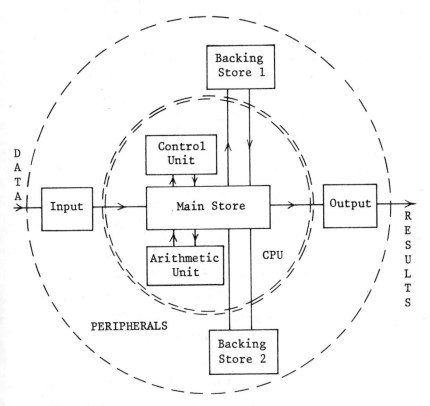

Fig. 1.1 The functional parts of a computer

1.4 *Control unit*

A program operates by directing the action of a part of the computer's central electronic circuits called the *control unit*; this extracts the instructions one-by-one in sequence from the store, decodes them, and initiates whatever action they indicate. The control unit regulates all other parts of the computer. In terms of their function these parts are: arithmetic unit, main store, backing stores, data input, and results output.[1] They are commonly grouped into the *central processing unit*, or *CPU* (control unit + arithmetic unit + main store), and the *peripherals* (input + output + backing stores) which surround it, as shown in Fig. 1.1.

The control unit appears in Fig. 1.1 but the program does not because it is not a physical part of the machine, and the figure shows only the *hardware* - that is, the electronic, electrical and mechanical units which together constitute the computer. The program is not a material thing, it is an idea, a plan, set down in the form of a description of the processes which the hardware is to carry out. Because they are not hardware, programs are referred to as *software*.

1.5 *Arithmetic unit*

The workshop of the CPU is its *arithmetic unit* which the control unit causes to perform a series of operations on the data, as instructed by the program. The name is a poor one for two reasons. First, its operations are not restricted to arithmetic only, for as well as adding, subtracting, multiplying and dividing the arithmetic unit can perform such *logical operation.* as comparing two items of data for identity, or to determine which is the larger, and it can perform a selection of the operations of *Boolean Algebra*.[2] For this reason the neutral term *data processing* is often used instead of 'calculation' or 'computation', for these have too strong a flavour of arithmetic.

Second, the data operated upon are not restricted to numbers only; they are just a string of bits which may represent a binary number, a packed decimal number, letters of an alphabet, weather map signs, machine tool control signals, or any other kind of symbol whatsoever. A moment's thought makes this clear, for to the arithmetic unit bits are bits, and have no meaning. Indeed, the very concept of having a meaning is anthropomorphic, and causes confusion when it is misapplied to a machine.

On a related point, the arithmetic unit does not 'do arithmetic', it switches and combines trains of electrical pulses according to rules that derive from the rules of arithmetic, in order to generate an output train which corresponds to the desired result: there is no mystery here, the entire process is purely mechanistic. The arithmetic unit simply does what our program instructs it to do to the set of bits that we choose to present to it. Whether or not its operations produce sense or nonsense depends on what we intended when we devised the program, and on our skill and accuracy in composing, writing down and checking the instructions in it; and it depends, also, on the relevance and accuracy of the input data. Computers have no inherent objection to converting rubbishy data into useless results.

Most computers have a set of instructions that allow groups of bits of a certain length to be handled more conveniently than groups of other lengths. These are the groups called *words*, and the number of bits in a computer's words, that is its *word length*, and the way in which these bits are allocated, determine the precision with which numerical data can be handled. Thus, a fairly typical word of 32 bits can handle 8-digit numbers in packed decimal form (up to about 100 millions), or binary numbers of 32 digits (about 4,300 millions). When the precision offered by one word is insufficient, adjacent words can be linked together for *double length* or *double precision* arithmetic. It is not blindingly obvious why this should ever be necessary, for 8-digit precision goes far beyond the needs of everyday life, and greatly exceeds the accuracy of most data. However, multiplying two 8-digit numbers produces a 16-digit number, and to keep this product within the capacity of the word it has to be cut down to its eight most significant digits, which introduces an error of about $\pm \frac{1}{2}$ in the last digit; and in calculations where a large number of successive multiplications is performed the errors can build up and become troublesome. Again, when a computation involves a relatively small difference between two large numbers these need to be precisely expressed if their calculated difference is to have any meaning at all. Nevertheless, we need at all times to remember that high precision does not necessarily mean high accuracy: thus, 3.1426789 states the value of π with 8-digit precision, but it has no more than 3-digit accuracy, because the last five figures are wrong. We shall be returning to this point in chapter 8, for it has especial relevance when dealing with economic data.

So far, we have been considering positive whole numbers, but many calculations also involve negative numbers and fractions. The sign can be indicated by allocating one bit of the word for this purpose, say, by using 0 for positive and 1 for negative. Fractional numbers can be handled provided we fix on a standard position for the location of the decimal (or binary) point. A common convention locates it at the extreme 'left-hand' end, which makes all numbers in the computer less than 1. In this *fixed point* working the programmer has to consider very carefully all the numbers in the computation - data, intermediate and final results alike, in order to scale them up or down so that they remain within the range of the largest number that can be represented: and he has to compute the appropriate re-scaling factor to apply to the result. If

8

he makes a mistake in scaling, some numbers may grow too large and *overflow* the capacity of the word; their most significant digits are then lost, and the rumps which remain are virtually meaningless. Electronic equipment is provided in the arithmetic unit to alert the operator should overflow occur; and fortunately its effects are usually pretty obvious.

The tedious and error-prone task of scaling can be avoided by using *floating point* representation. In this, the word is divided into two parts. The first part 'a' is a fraction called the *mantissa*, or *fixed point part*; and the second part 'b' is an integer called the *characteristic*, or the *exponent*. Thus, in *floating decimal* a decimal number 'D' is represented by the formula $D = a \times 10^{b}$, where 'a' and 'b' can be positive or negative numbers. For instance, 368,700 would appear as 0.3687,06; and 0.00234 as 0.234, -02. Note that the fractional part is *normalized*, that is, scaled so that space is not wasted by leading zeros.

Floating point representation is not restricted to decimal numbers. In *floating binary* the binary number 'B' is represented as $B = a \times 2^{b}$: and, a byte-oriented computer may employ *floating hexadecimal*, in which one byte of the word is used for the sign of the number and its exponent, and the other bytes for the mantissa, and then $H = a \times 16^{b}$.

There is some loss of precision when using floating point because the precision depends on the mantissa, and only 'a' of the word's (a + b) digits are available to it. Double length working can be used with floating point when extra precision is necessary. However, providing the exponent is not too small it is possible to cover a range of magnitudes wide enough to make scaling unnecessary for most purposes — a range from 10^{60} to 10^{-60} is not uncommon; and, for this reason, floating point working is universal for non-specialist programmers.

There is a risk that when two very small numbers are multiplied they may generate a product which is too small to be represented by the available exponent; this tiresome situation is known as *underflow* and in some machines it is automatically detected and notified to the operator. Numbers that are too small to be represented are commonly replaced by zero, and the usual floating point representation of zero is zeros in all bit positions in the word.

1.6 *Main store*

The arithmetic unit contains some one-word stores called *registers*, but it is the third part of the CPU - the *Main Store* which has the principal task of holding the program, and also current data and partly finished results. The main store is divided into pigeon holes called *locations* each able to hold one word, and each identified by a number known as its *address*. In most designs the speed of this store sets the speed of the computer, for instructions cannot be obeyed faster than the store can produce them and the necessary data. Until recently main stores consisted of arrays of many thousands of tiny rings, or *cores*, of magnetic material threaded on flat co-ordinate grids or *planes* of wires in an arrangement that resembled a set of bead mats. Each core could be magnetized either clockwise or anti-clockwise and was thus able to store one bit. Core stores are giving way to compact arrays of miniature electronic circuits produced on thin slices of crystalline silicon by automatic masking, printing and etching processes, because this *solid state*, or *integrated circuit*, technology offers higher speed at lower cost.

Main stores are costly items, and the capacity and speed of the store provided depends on the power required, and on the acceptable cost of the computer. Commercially available computers range from Mini's costing as little as £1000, up to

massive systems costing more than £3 millions. Typical main
stores have capacities in the range 4000 to 10 million bytes,*
and can produce the contents of any specified location after
a delay of from 0.2 to 2 μS, where 1 μS (pronounced micro-
second) = 1/1,000,000th second. The corresponding computers
execute their programs at rates of 500 thousand to 50 million
instructions a second. These rates seem to be incredibly high
compared with the 20 seconds which we require to copy and add
together two 8-digit numbers, but before we are too impressed
let us recall that computers proceed in very much tinier steps
than we do, so that they may need 10, or 100, or even 1000 instructions to complete what we seem to achieve as a unit operation. Even so, they are left with a handsome margin of advantage in both time and cost; moreover, they very rarely make
processing errors. The truly splendid 'computer mistakes'
that hit the headlines are almost always caused by human error.
Either incorrect data have been put in, leading to a *GIGO* -
garbage in garbage out, situation; or, their operator has
moved the wrong control, or the right one at the wrong time;
or, their programmer has failed to find and correct all the
errors and inadequacies in his program.

1.7 *Peripherals*

     In commercial work particularly, extremely large amounts
of data have to be handled. For example, to prepare its telephone bills the Post Office must maintain and process a file
of data which has a substantial entry for each of its several
millions of telephone customers. It would be quite impractical
and ruinously expensive to keep so large a file, amounting to
several thousands of Megabytes, in the main store of a computer,

---

* Usually written: 4kB to 10 MB, where k (kilo) often stands
for the 'binary thousand' 1024, and M (Mega) for 1024 × 1024.

and this store is, therefore, extended by much cheaper peripheral *backing stores* which record the data on magnetic tapes, disks or drums. These are discussed in more detail in chapter 3, but we may note that, because these peripherals are somewhat elephantine electrical mechanisms with ponderous moving parts, their speeds are very much slower than that of the electronic main store. This large difference in speed offers scope for the exercise of forethought and ingenuity in program design in order to minimize the extent to which the slow backing stores hold up the main process. Fig. 1 shows only two backing stores, but a large computer may be equipped with one or two magnetic drums, plus two or three sets of magnetic disks, plus six or more tape units.

Commercial computers are rather like construction toys, for the buyer can choose to have more or less main store, and as many peripherals as he is likely to be able to afford. Thus, Intergalactic Computers Model T is the name of a kit, and two of their Model T's will be identical only if they happen to have precisely the same *configuration* of optional items. When (as is usually the case) their configurations differ there will be limitations on the extent to which work can be switched from one machine to the other.

Data and programs have to be brought into a computer system through its *input units*, and the results are delivered by its *output units*. For each of these there is a wide range of alternatives, as we shall see in chapters 2 and 3, and it is enough now to note that the 'throughput' of work can be sadly throttled back if inadequate input units starve the computer of data, or if the output units become congested with the rush of results. Moreover, it is at their input and output units that we meet our computers face to face, and it is important, therefore, that these units should accept our data and present their results to us in ways that we find convenient and com-

prehensible, and not - as has too often happened - be designed
primarily to achieve mechanical efficiency within themselves,
or economy in their manufacture.

1.8   *The computer at work*

We have now reviewed the items that make up a computer,
and it remains to illustrate how they work together. The illustration is based on a highly-simplified commercial job in
which the objective is to 'up-date' the stock record of a
supermarket in terms of recent sales and deliveries. The
stock file is recorded on an exchangeable magnetic disk pack
(see par. 3.2.3), and it lists for each item of goods: its
identification code, the quantity in stock, and the re-ordering level. The operator begins by loading the pack of disks
that contains this file onto a specified disk drive unit in
the backing store. The item codes and quantities of each of
the sales and deliveries transactions are recorded on a reel
of magnetic tape in chronological order, just as they occurred,
and the operator loads this reel onto a specified tape unit in
the backing store. He then checks that the printer which has
been designated to print the results is loaded with sufficient
of the specified stationery.

The next step is to feed the program for the job into the
computer's main store. This program is recorded on a pack of
punched cards, and the operator loads these into the feed hopper of a specified card reader - one of the peripheral input
units. He then uses another peripheral input unit, the electric typewriter on his control desk, to send a coded instruction to the control unit. This instruction transfers control
of the computer to the first instruction of a loading program
that is permanently stored in the machine, and the loading program starts the card reader and causes the instructions of the
stock control program to be placed in successive, known, loca-

tions of the main store. When all the cards have been read the loader program uses the electric typewriter to notify the operator that it has run to completion, and that control has been returned to him. Often the operator's commands to the computer are printed in black on the typewriter's paper, and the computer's responses are printed in red, and in this way a complete log of their interaction is kept. The operator next enters another coded instruction which transfers control to the first instruction of the stock control program.

This program causes the CPU to read the first transaction record from the magnetic tape, and to compare its item code with successive entries in the old stock file until it finds a match. The transaction quantity is then added to the old stock if it is coded as a delivery, or subtracted if it is a sale. The next transaction record is then read from the tape and the process repeated until every transaction has been dealt with. Thus, the program is fed in once only at the start of the job, but it is used repeatedly - once for each trans-action; so if there were 2000 transactions then the program would be executed 2000 times when the file was up-dated (per-haps daily) and clearly it must be both accurate and efficient. Finally, the now up-dated stock file is scanned item by item, and for each the revised stock is compared with the re-ordering level. Where the stock exceeds this level the program skips on, but where it falls short the record is copied out by the output printer. In this way the printer lists those items, and only those, that call for re-ordering action by the shop manager. When every item has been scanned the program notifies the operator that it has run to completion, and so that pro-cessing is complete. The process is set out as a *flow chart* in Fig. 1.2; it may seem to be a long-winded one, and computers do indeed tackle their work in a plodding, pedestrian fashion - but they plod away at very high speed indeed. The program we

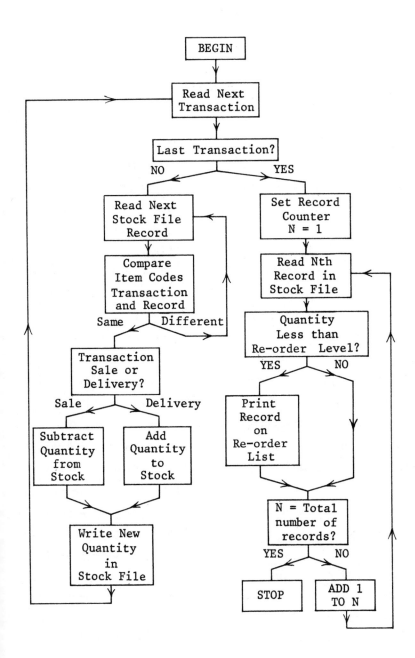

Fig. 1.2 Flow chart

15

have been considering is not the only one that would update this file, nor is it necessarily the best. Each program does one job only; but a given job can be done by any of a number of alternative programs.

1.9 *Computer decisions*

In producing the printed action list of our example the computer — or rather its program — 'took the decisions' whether or not a particular item should be ordered. Some timid souls have found this to be a most sinister fact, and in a panic they have made wild extrapolations to the point where computers are taking all the important business decisions, and men are bypassed. However, in the example the computer's 'decision' was taken exactly as specified by the instructions which *we* laid down in its program, with no scope for the exercise of independence or initiative, two more words that are inapplicable when speaking of machines. It is, of course, true that among the bottom levels of any large bureaucracy the staff, also, are required to decide strictly according to rigid rules, and are allowed no room to exercise discretion; but this implies only that the staff are forced to act as machines, and not that computers are usurping any proper role of men and women. It explains also why so many clerical and low-level managerial tasks can easily be transferred to computers. The fact that computers work strictly to rule implies that the writing of programs is a much more exacting task than the writing of rules for human beings; nothing can be left to common sense, the machine does precisely what it has been told to do, and no more, rather than what we may have intended; and carelessness and lack of foresight can produce some quite absurd side effects.

Although we have no cause for alarm in the programmed decisions taken by computers, the fact that they can adapt and vary their action according to the data they receive or the results they produce is very valuable. It means, for instance, that we do not have to write separate individual programs for each item of data processed; we can write a program that covers all known possibilities and use programmed tests and decisions to allow the computer to select that path through the general program which fits the particular circumstances of the data it encounters.

Programmed control is not unique to computers: even washing machines and central heating systems can be programmed to suit our needs. The extra ingredient that computers have is *stored-program control*, for they hold their current programs in their main stores in binary form. The programs share these stores with data, and just as the data can be operated upon by the arithmetic unit so also can the instructions in the programs be modified by arithmetical and logical operations. This most usefully enables programs to be greatly condensed. For example, to read in and put away 1000 items of data in successive locations of the main store we could write a rather uninspired program of 2001 instructions thus:

(1)   Read in Item 1

(2)   Store in Location 1001

(3)   Read in Item 2

(4)   Store in Location 1002

....

....

(1999) Read in Item 1000

(2000) Store in Location 2000

(2001) Stop

This method of setting down every instruction to be obeyed is known as *straight line coding* - *coding* being the programmer's term for the writing down of instructions. But, our ability to modify instructions by operating on them as if they were data allows us to condense this elementary program from 2001 to 8 instructions, thus:

(1)   Set T = 1001
(2)   Set N = 1
(3)   Read in Item N
(4)   Store in Location 1000 + N
(5)   Set N = N + 1
(6)   If N = T, then jump to Instruction (8)
(7)   Jump to Instruction (3)
(8)   Stop

Five points arise from this example. First, Instruction (4) is modified by changing the address of the main store location to which it applies, but the function performed, namely 'store', is unchanged. It is, in fact, possible to modify either the function part or the address part of an instruction, or both, but *address modification* is much the more common in practice. Second, in our example the address is modified by simply adding one, that is by counting, but it is equally possible to add (or subtract) whatever number has been placed for that purpose in a special one-word store known as an *index register*; and a large computer may have 8 or more such registers holding a choice of relevant numbers. Third, the revised version of the program takes the form of a *loop* of five instructions which are performed repeatedly until a prescribed condition (N=T=1001) is satisfied; and the program can be easily adapted to any other number of items by simply altering the value of T in Instruction (1). Looping is a common and invaluable program technique: indeed without the condensation which loops make possible it would hardly be feasible to write down instructions as fast as computers can consume them, and it would be far too costly to hold programs

18

in the main store as straight line coding. Fourth, the looping cycle is terminated when the condition specified in Instruction (6) is met; this instruction is one of those that give computers their apparent power of decision. They are known as *conditional jump* or *conditional branch* instructions because when their specified condition is satisfied the program *jumps* out of its current sequence and runs along an alternative branch line. Some other examples of conditional jump instructions are:

    Jump to N if A = 0
    Jump to N if A ≠ 0*
    Jump to N if A > 0*
    Jump to N if A < 0*

where A is the current result in the arithmetic unit (the accumulator), and N is the number of the first instruction of the new branch to be followed. Fifth, Instruction (7) is an *unconditional jump* which simply specifies the next (out of sequence) instruction to be obeyed. The importance of jump instructions of both kinds can be judged from the fact that on average about one-third of the instructions actually obeyed in executing a program are jumps, and that this proportion may reach 60% in some types of program.

1.10 *Four key features*
    To sum up, four features characterize computers.
(a) Control by exchangeable programs: this allows us to set up a computer quickly and easily to execute any of a wide variety of data processing tasks.

---

* ≠ means 'not equal to'; > means 'greater than'; < means 'less than'; in each case the wide end is next to the larger quantity.

(b) Location of the program in the Main Store: this enables us to modify its instructions in the course of execution and thus to abbreviate our programs and adapt them to whatever circumstances we can foresee may arise.

(c) Conditional Jump Instructions: these allow us to write our program for the general case by using jumps to select the appropriate parts of the general program for each item processed.

(d) High processing speed at low cost: this allows us to undertake computations and processes otherwise too lengthy to be either feasible or economic.

These features may not appear to be very exciting, nor is any of them at all mysterious, but it is from them and from the ingenuity of their programmers that computers derive their striking power over an extremely diverse range of applications.

1.11 *Bibliography*

A general description of computer hardware and software is to be found in:

(1) *Electronic Computers*, by S.H. Hollingdale and G.C.Tootill Penguin Books, 2nd edn with revisions 1975.

And a useful glossary of about 3000 terms, with some general articles, is in:

(2) *A Dictionary of Computers*, by Anthony Chandor *et al.* Penguin Books, 1970.

The representation of numbers in a computer is discussed in another book in this series:

(3) *Information Representation and Manipulation in a Computer* by E.S. Page and L.B. Wilson. Cambridge University Press, 1973.

See also in this series:

(4) *Computing Systems Hardware*, by M. Wells. Cambridge University Press, 1976.

EXAMPLES 1

(1.1) Compare the numbers of bits needed to represent 7963 in
   (a) an alpha-numeric code using one 8-bit byte for each
   character,
   (b) packed decimal form,
   (c) pure binary.

(1.2) Write down the floating decimal and the floating binary
   representations of : (a) 69,632; (b) 1024; (c) 0.0625.

(1.3) Giving your reasons, say how you would expect the quantity 21 hours 19 minutes 12.8 seconds to be represented in
   a computer
   (a) if it were merely to be stored and reproduced as a
   part of a larger record,
   (b) if it is to be used in calculation.

(1.4) For a binary computer with a word-length of 24 bits,
   show how floating point numbers can be represented, and
   indicate the operations involved in (a) multiplying,
   (b) adding two such numbers.

(1.5) Distinguish between the C.P.U. and the peripherals of a
   computer installation, and explain what conditions have
   to be met for two computers to have the same configuration.

(1.6) List the reasons that may make it difficult to transfer
   data and programs from one computer to another.

(1.7) Distinguish between conditional and unconditional Jump
   instructions. Indicate where you would expect to find each
   used in a program corresponding to the flow chart of Fig.
   1.2.

(1.8) For the file updating program outlined in par. 1.8, say
   by reference to the flow chart (Fig. 1.2) what you would
   expect to happen if, in error:
   (a) the magnetic tape used contained transactions re-

lating to a quite different program,

(b) the magnetic tape corresponded to the program, but last month's transaction tape were used instead of the current one; can you suggest how this mishap might be prevented?

(1.9) 'We need not fear the taking of decisions by computers, for they are limited to routine matters only, and decide strictly as they have been programmed.' Comment on this statement, and criticize its implications.

(1.10) Explain the importance of being able to perform operations on instructions as if they were data, and give examples of the usefulness of modifying:

(a) the address part,

(b) the function part,

of an instruction.

2 · The input of data

2.1 *Introduction*

Data do not make up the whole of computer input; programs have to be put into the main store and control messages stream between the operator and the CPU. Nevertheless, data are by far the largest part of input, and the means and methods required for data are used for programs and for control messages also. In terms of sheer volume, and hence of equipment sales, the input for commercial data processing* greatly exceeds the rest and sets the operating and design standards in common use. The stumbling crudity of the methods used to prepare data for input to a computer contrast strikingly with the swift elegance of its central electronics; this and the bewildering variety of techniques being used, serve to remind us that the craft of computing is still in a very early stage of its development – an encouraging thought for computer scientists.

2.2 *The importance of input*

With the rare exceptions of such universal constants as e or π, and of sets of random or quasi-random numbers generated internally by specialized hardware or software for use in statistical programs, data enter the computer from outside. The nature and quality of this inflow of data very largely deter-

---

* 'Commercial data processing' here, and hereafter, means the use of computers in commercial management and accounting, and in government offices.

mine what results a program can produce, for no amount of clever processing can convert sow's ears into silk purses. Again, in chapter 10 we shall look at the threat to our individual privacy which is posed by the processing of detailed personal records by computers. Many subtle and ingenious methods of protection have been proposed but our fundamental and absolute control is over the supply of input data, for what does not go in cannot come out.

In commercial data processing the input of data is a very expensive activity which can account for as much as 50% of the total cost of computing. It can occupy a large staff of keyboard operators who require office space, and who consume substantial amounts of electrical energy for lighting and heating and to drive their machines. We may note in passing that all this expenditure of time and money does not itself advance the processing of the data, indeed it exposes it to the risk of errors; it merely prepares the data for processing by transcribing it from one physical carrier to another, for instance from a written document to a magnetic tape. Failure to get the input system right can ruin the economics of commercial data processing, and the design skills needed for success are not those of computing only - work study and personnel management are equally important, for the efficient control of data preparation staff, and of the irregular and peaky flow of large volumes of documents is no mean problem.

The prime importance of input data makes it essential that they should be:

(a) relevant, for otherwise confusion will result; moreover, expensive storage capacity will be wasted;

(b) complete, for otherwise processing will be brought to a halt;

(c) accurate, if the results are to be acceptably free from errors;

(d) appropriately precise, neither reducing the inherent
accuracy of the facts they represent, nor lending a
spurious precision to the results;

(e) identified, sequenced and arranged as specified by the
programmer for the computer will deal with each item as
its program expects to encounter it, and cannot recognise
an unknown, or reshape an incorrectly structured, input;

(f) received from an authorized source, for otherwise invalid
data may be used to produce consequences not intended by
the programmer, or for purposes not acceptable to those
they concern; for example, to pry into confidential files,
or to alter or erase their contents.

2.3 *Character recognition*

How nice it would be if we were able to speak or write to
our computers quite naturally and with no more constraint on
our vocabulary, syntax or sequence of ideas than we observe in
ordinary conversation. However, the problem of how to translate our free expression into regimented groups of bits in a
computer store is largely unsolved. In essence, the problem
is one of pattern recognition, a backward area generally, and
we simply do not know how to describe the nature or specify
the key properties of the patterns that underlie and inform our
speech and handwriting. Hence, we are not able to set down
the rules by which these patterns can be recognized, and as
Lady Lovelace pointed out more than a century ago a computer
can do only whatever we know how to order it to perform.
Direct spoken input to a computer is a commonplace of science
fiction, but it has so far been demonstrated only for nursery
vocabularies of the ten decimal numerals and a few command
words, and has therefore found little practical application.

The reading of handwriting can be difficult even for men
and women, and those computers that do attempt it wisely con-

fine themselves to numerals. Moreover, they require these to be written on standard documents within pre-printed 'boxes' that serve to locate and align them precisely, and which also control their size. Our numerals were clearly not designed for easy recognition by machines. When carelessly written they are liable to be confused with one another; thus, a 3 with incurving tips resembles a broken 8; 1 and 7, 5 and 6 are open to similar confusion. The reading of machine-printed material is much easier, for its size, location, shape and density are all less variable. Even so, the wide range of type fonts, and of paper sizes, colours and qualities, adds considerably to the difficulty of handling and reading ordinary printed matter, and in practice automatic reading is confined to specially-prepared documents printed in one of the type fonts designed to simplify the task of *character recognition*. The aim is to strike a balance between our convenience and simplicity in the machine; but in some cases rather too many concessions have been made to the machine, and the resulting print can confuse an unpractised reader – as, for example, the ugly style used for numerical information on cheques. These numbers are intended to inform the bank's staff rather than the public at large, and they do not therefore need to be universally understood. Where no untrained man or woman needs to read the information, machine-reading can be further assisted by using a *bar code* or a *dot code* in which letters and numerals are represented by groups of printed lines or dots.

Document readers sense characters printed in ordinary black ink by scanning them with photo-electric cells which convert variations in the reflected light into electrical impulses. This method is known as *optical character recognition (OCR)*, and two fonts, *OCR A* and *OCR B*, have been standardized internationally. The photo cells respond also to adventitious marks on the paper caused by dirt, creases, endorsements, signatures and so forth. Two methods are used to combat this.

The first, used where human reading is not required, prints a dot or a bar code in an ink that phosporesces under ultraviolet light, and dirt and overmarking do not. A much more common method is to print the characters in an ink which contains iron oxides; the ink is black and can be read by eye, but it can also be magnetized and sensed in the same way as the magnetic tape in a domestic sound recorder. The technique is called *magnetic ink character recognition (MICR)* and the numerals on cheques are printed in this way. Once again, dirt, creases, and overmarking rarely contain magnetic materials. The output from an optical or magnetic character reader is a group of bits for each character which passes under the reading head.

As we have noted, the problems of automatic reading test the limits of our knowledge, for we have little understanding of the ways in which we ourselves recognize patterns - how we isolate and define the invariant core that persists throughout a wide range of transformations, distortions, displacements, incompletenesses and masking. However, there are substantial problems also at the much less elevated level of practical engineering, for paper sheets are poor stuff when it comes to rapid movement by machine. Their quality is variable; on damp days they grow limp and crumple, and on dry days they electrify and stick together, and in either case they jam the feed mechanism. Paper is abrasive and causes wear; it produces dust which unerringly migrates to the oilier parts of the machine. Because our documents are designed for human hands and eyes, they are very much larger than would be needed to convey the same amount of data to a photocell or magnetic head, and this means that paper-handling mechanisms tend to be large, noisy and hot. Their salesmen seek to persuade by an awed recital of tens of thousands of documents handled in an hour: the appropriate response is honest disbelief that so many horse-power are employed to move such minute quantities of magnetic or printer's ink.

2.4 *Mark sensing and scanning*

The difficulties of automatic reading have led to most computer input being transcribed by methods which avoid the problems of pattern recognition, or which leave them with human eyes and brains. Thus, input data can be recorded by making simple marks (strokes) in alternative positions on pre-printed documents of standard sizes; the automatic reader then merely has to detect the presence or absence of a mark. In *mark scanning* it does this optically by reflected light; in *mark sensing* a graphite pencil is used to make the mark, which can then be detected by its ability to conduct electricity. The documents may themselves be printed in a previous run on the computer, then circulated to initiate some action outside the computer system - for instance, the payment of a bill - and returned after marking as an input to the next run. Papers of this kind are called *turn around* documents, and they risk the by now traditional maltreatment of folding, spindling or mutilation. In these documents, such standard data as name, address, and account number can be pre-printed in order to ensure that they are entered without the risk of transcription errors.

2.5 *Keyboard input*

Keyboards are a popular way of leaving the problems of character recognition with men and women, and various methods are available for transcribing data from written or printed material.

(a) Direct electrical input from a console typewriter, or from a local or remote *visual display unit, (VDU)* which combines a keyboard and a television-like cathode-ray-tube screen. The print out or display shows the operator what he or she has keyed, so that it can be checked by proof-reading, and immediately corrected. For complicated data entries a VDU can display on its screen the equivalent of a form to be filled in, with boxes of appropriate lengths for each *field*; that is, for each separate item of the data. This *format control* reduces errors as well as helping to ensure that the data enter in the order and arrangement specified by the programmer.

(b) A keyboard can control electrically driven mechanisms that punch holes into a strip of paper tape or a card.

(i) *Paper tape* commonly comes in reels of 1000 ft (300 m), 1 in. (25 mm) wide. Each character is recorded as a single 'row' of holes across the tape, each hole corresponding to one bit in the code that represents the character. Successive rows are spaced 0.1 in. (2.5 mm) apart, and there may be 5, 6, 7 or 8 holes in a row. There is an *International Standards Organization (ISO)* code for 8-track paper tape which allocates 7 holes to the character code and uses the 8th hole for checking. The presence or absence of a hole in the tape is sensed photoelectrically, and input data rates of 1000 char./sec. (8000 bits/sec.) are usual. Paper tape finds its main application where relatively small volumes of data are being handled. Unchecked keypunched material typically contains 2 or 3 errors per 1000 characters, which must be corrected before the tape is presented to a computer. A second operator therefore takes the first operator's tape and the documents from which the data were transcribed, and inserts the tape into a machine called a *verifier*. This compares the tape character-by-character with what the second operator is trying to enter through the verifier's keyboard. When the two agree the character is punched into a second 'verified' tape: when they differ the verifier's keyboard locks, then having decided which is wrong the operator unlocks the keyboard and enters the correct character into the verified tape. For convenience the two tapes usually have a different colour, say red for unchecked danger and white for verified purity. Verification reduces the number of errors to 1 per 100,000 or less depending on the skill and care of the operators and the legibility of the original documents; it cannot, of course, correct errors present in those documents.

(ii)   The most common size of *punched card* is $7\frac{3}{8}$ in. × $3\frac{1}{4}$ in. (188 × 82 mm) divided lengthwise into 80 columns each with 12 punching positions; normally each column is used to represent one character. Punched cards can be read at rates of 600 to 1200 cards per minute (5600 to 11,200 bits/sec.). Alternatively, we can use all 80 × 12 punching positions for binary data and obtain a capacity of 960 bits per card; this increases the input data rate to some 10 to 20 thousand bits/ sec. Many different kinds of machine are available for hand- ling punched cards, thus, they can be counted, sorted, two packs can be merged by interleaving their cards after compari- son, and the whole or parts of the data in the cards can be listed, totalled or tabulated. Punched cards have been the most popular method of input, and a large proportion of the data that have entered computers has been punched into cards. Even in the early 1970's, about two-thirds of computer input came from punched cards; however, this proportion is declining and cards can be expected to disappear – but not quickly.

(iii)   Data can be transcribed into machine-readable form by using a typewriter that prints with an ordinary black ribbo in one of the standard OCR fonts. This method has the merit o using ordinary typing skills and cheap keyboard machines, both of which are more generally available than those required for punching tapes or cards. However, much more attention has to be paid to accuracy, and to correct layout, than is normal for ordinary commercial typing. Similarly, the variable data on cheques (the amount) is copied from the drawer's handwritten entry onto the cheque itself by operators using keyboard machines called *magnetic ink encoders*.

(iv) Battery-driven portable units are available in which data are entered through a small keyboard, curtailed to handle numbers and a few symbols only, and are recorded on a cassette tape similar to those used for domestic sound recording. An electronic notebook of this kind can hold 500,000 characters on one cassette, and reproduce them at rather more than 1000 char./sec. It is suitable for use by gas and electricity meter readers, and in scientific or survey work where data have to be recorded in the field.

2.6 *Indirect input*

The methods described above use paper or cassette tapes, or cards, as the *medium* which carries the data, and the physical difficulties of handling these media limit them to input data rates of 1000 to 2000 char./sec., say 8 to 16 k bit/sec. Within a computer data flow over the *highway* that links its main store to the registers in its arithmetic unit, and to the peripherals, at rates up to several Megabits/sec. Clearly, with this great disparity in speed processing would be greatly hampered if it had to wait for a single, slow input mechanism. Three methods are used to counter this source of inefficiency:

(a) A computer can be programmed to accept data from more than one input device, to copy it onto a magnetic tape or disk in the backing store, and to do so concurrently with processing data that it has taken in already. This is called: Simultaneous Peripheral Operations Off-line or *Spooling*. The tape or disk record is then available for subsequent processing, when it can yield up its data at rates as high as 500 k bit/sec.

(b) As we shall see in chapter 5, a computer can run several
     independent programs concurrently, and one of these may
     be one that reads data from a group of input peripherals
     into the main store for early attention by the processing
     program. Usually, each slow input unit is connected to
     a *buffer* register which it fills at its own pace, but
     which when full is rapidly emptied into the main store:
     this allows the computer to allocate only brief, infre-
     quent intervals of its time to the input unit, and to
     apply the rest to other processes. The buffer may be a
     part of the input unit's hardware, or it may be an area
     of the main store reserved for this purpose, or which
     has been so earmarked by the programmer.

(c) Clearly, the high data transfer rates of magnetic tapes
     and disks can be made available more directly by record-
     ing data on them straight from a keyboard. Until recently
     this has been neither practicable nor economic. The pract
     ical difficulties arose because the rows of magnetized
     spots that represent a character on a computer tape may be
     spaced 1/500th of an inch (0.05 mm) or less apart, and the
     mechanical problems of advancing a flexible tape by so
     small an amount between key strokes are quite severe. The
     economic problem arose because a computer tape unit is
     both expensive and hopelessly under-utilized when tied to
     the snail's pace of a single keyboard. One solution uses
     a much less densely recorded tape, which is later copied
     automatically onto standard computer tape. Another is *Key*
     to-Disk equipment which uses a cheap 'mini-computer' to
     link 10 or more operators to one magnetic disk. The mini
     also performs a wide and subtle range of checking, veri-
     fying and editing functions, alerts the operator when
     errors are detected and rechecks the corrected entry. When
     transcription is complete the data are copied onto standar

magnetic tapes or exchangeable disks in whatever code and
format has been specified. Statistics are produced to
monitor performance, and it is claimed that operator productivity is 10 to 14% higher, and errors fewer, than for
a single keypunch operation.

2.7 *Data capture at source*

The error-prone and expensive hand transcription of data
is eliminated when data can be put into electronic form at
their point of origin. This is the normal situation when computers are used to control manufacturing processes for the input data are supplied by automatic instruments measuring temperatures, pressures, rates of fluid flow and so on. In traffic
control systems, data are supplied directly from pressure pads
in the roadway, and the operation of traffic signals is monitored. Automatic monitoring is used to check the flow of water
in rivers, and the flows of gas and electricity at various
points in the main feeders of their distribution networks. In
each case the captured data are fed directly into a central computer which logs them, and tests for various kinds of irregularity in order to initiate automatic corrective action or to
raise an alarm. Process control and monitoring are discussed
in chapter 9.

In some kinds of commercial data processing also, data can
be generated as a by-product of a main activity. For example,
the electrical cash registers of a supermarket may be directly
connected to a magnetic tape recorder which captures data about
the quantities and types of goods sold and the cash taken. Or
again, in a branch bank the cash dispensing machine may be linked directly to the bank's central computer in order to check the
validity of a customer's credit card, and to confirm that his
account has a sufficient balance to meet his demand for cash.
At one stage removed, we have the sales tags attached to garm-

ents, which record data by punched holes or notches; the tags
are detached when the garment is sold and fed later into the
hopper of an automatic reader connected to the computer which
is processing the sales analysis, stock control and accounting programs.

2.8 *Graphical input*

So far, we have been considering data in the form of
strings of numerals or letters; but in engineering and architectural design, in meteorology, in cartography and in town
planning many data arise in graphical form. To be stored by
a computer such data have to be 'digitized' by being converted
into the coordinates which specify the positions of all key
points on the diagram. The most common way of doing this is
to display the diagram on a large cathode-ray tube screen, and
for the operator to apply a *light pen* to each of the key point
in turn. The light pen consists of a photocell mounted at the
tip of a holder the size of a fountain pen, and connected by
cable to the computer; the photocell detects the light signal
from the screen. As well as recording the coordinates, the
light pen can be used to command the computer to call up a
program able to trace straight or curved lines between selecte
points on the screen in order to draw a diagram on it.

2.9 *Data transmission*

For a computer that serves a single university, or a research laboratory, or which controls a manufacturing plant, th
data arise in its immediate neighbourhood; but in most commercial applications, in traffic control and in the monitoring o
distribution networks, the data have to be collected over lon
distances. When immediacy is essential for operational reaso
as in traffic control, and where it can be justified on econor
grounds, as in airline seat reservation, then the data can be
transmitted through telecommunication channels in the cable o

radio links of the telephone authority. The usual channels vary in capacity from about 100 to 48,000 bits/sec., but it is not difficult to provide capacities of several Megabits/sec. - the problems are economic not technological. The most ubiquitous channel is the ordinary dialled-up telephone connection in the 'public switched network', and these channels can be used to transmit data at rates up to about 5000 bits/sec. Almost all data channels are provided in an established network which was designed to suit the telephone rather than the different and in some ways more exacting requirements of data, and errors can be introduced by the pick up of electrical noise and interference. A great deal of ingenuity has been applied to the invention of codes and of equipment designed to minimize these errors, and it is possible to reduce them to any desired level, except when the channel is obviously faulty. Naturally this cannot be done without cost, and there is no point in attempting to reduce the transmission errors much below the level of those inherent in the original data supplied for transmission. The design of data transmission networks is a specialist subject;[1] it involves substantial questions of policy[3] as well as of technique: and it is a matter of increasing importance to the effective use of computers.

2.10 *Checking*

The need for accuracy in the input data can hardly be overstated, for on this depends the value of the results produced by processing it. We have touched already on the verification of data produced by keypunches, on proof-reading to check data intended for optical or magnetic character reading, and on the coding and equipment techniques used to control data transmission errors. None of these can detect or reduce errors in the original data, as when someone has misplaced the decimal point, or written metres when kilometres is appropriate, or transposed adjacent digits. It is, therefore, very necessary to check the input data, and *data vet* programs occupy a considerable amount of the time of any computer used for commercial or industrial purposes. A very nice judgement indeed is required to determine how far data vetting should be taken, for in the limit it can cost more than it can save. The vetting of data includes checking for transcription accuracy, and testing for validity and credibility.

Transcription accuracy is checked by *control totals* which are best illustrated by an example. Thus, a clerk preparing a batch of invoices for processing uses a desk calculator to work out the total cash sum invoiced for the whole batch, and he sends his *batch total* to the data preparation room with his invoices. The total will be punched into a card that is prefixed to the corresponding pack of cards, and when these are later input to the computer its data-vet program will re-compute the batch total and compare it with the prefixed total. If they are different, then the batch of cards is referred back to the punch operators for the error to be found and corrected. Any numerical data can be totalled in this way; sometimes the total has no meaning, as when dates of birth are totalled, and it is then known as a *hash total*. A classic hash total was that of the beggar whose appeal board bore the legend: 'Wounds 4, wives 2, children 8, Total 14'. Computer data often include identifying numbers, for instance part-numbers for engineering stores items, and these can be protected against errors by having a *check digit* added to them. In one system, called a *Modulo-N* check, the identifying number is divided by N, and the remainder used as the check digit which is tacked onto the end. On input, the data vet program re-computes the check digit and tests it against its input value.

The validity of an entry can be checked by testing to see

whether it is complete, whether each unit of data in it occurs in the specified sequence, whether it has the correct number of characters, and whether these are of the right kinds, letters or numerals as the case may be. Credibility checking covers such matters as testing that in a date the day of the month does not exceed 31, or that some item has not a misplaced decimal point – thus, it is not credible that 250 hours of overtime should have been worked by one man in one week. Credibility checking can be quite subtle, and its design is an interesting intellectual exercise, but care is needed, as an example will serve to indicate. The data vet program of an air-cargo system was being designed to reject the entry of data relating to imports that did not match the circumstances of their airports of origin, for instance bananas from Iceland, until it was remembered that aircraft are sometimes diverted.

2.11 *Bibliography*

The frantic pace of development of data input equipment induces a state of chronic obsolescence which makes it necessary to check the details of its performance with the manufacturers.

The subject of data transmission spans two independent disciplines, and balanced accounts are scarce: however, there is a comprehensive treatment of the subject by two experienced practitioners in :

(1)   *Communication Networks for Computers*, by D.W. Davies and D.L.A. Barber.   John Wiley, 1973.

See also:

(2)   *Computing Systems Hardware*, by M. Wells.   Cambridge University Press, 1976.

Your author, too, has dealt briefly with the principles, and touched on the policy questions raised, in:

(3)   *Computers, Communications and Society*, by Murray Laver. Oxford University Press, 1975.

(2.1) State what criteria you would use to determine the relevance of items proposed as input data for a program; and apply your criteria to the following items as possible input data to a factory payroll program: Surname, Christian names, sex, marital status, date of birth, place of birth, address, branch bank code, pay number, factory department, job title, sick absence record, religion, trade union membership number. What relevant data are missing?

(2.2) List the reasons which make it difficult to design an automatic machine to recognise either (a) handwriting or (b) spoken numerals.

(2.3) On the basis of one byte per character, compare the storage densities in bits/cm^2 of: (a) 8-track paper tape, (b) 80-column punched cards – one column per character, (c) 80-column punched cards – binary punched, (d) a page of this book, as a possible input to a character reader, (e) standard 9-track magnetic tape – 12 mm wide and 32 bits/mm.

(2.4) The Bible contains 774,000 words, or 4.3 million characters when the spaces between words are included. Assuming one byte per character where appropriate, how long would be required to transmit the entire contents of The Bible between two places 100 miles apart: (a) by teleprinter, at 50 words/min., (b) by telephoned dictation at 120 words/min., (c) by first class post, (d) by motor cycle courier, (e) by data transmission over a telephone channel at 5 k bit/sec., (f) over a wideband data link at 48 k bit/sec? Repeat the calculations for a data input message of 500 bits, and draw up a table comparing the two cases. What conclusions does it suggest?

(2.5) Write brief notes on three different ways in which the problems of automatic pattern recognition can be avoided in the input of data to computer.

(2.6) Computer data are organized in units of ascending size, thus: bits, bytes, characters, words, fields, records, reels (or disks), and files. Define these units and show the relationship between them.

(2.7) In the input of data to a computer distinguish between verification and vetting. Give an example to show how it is feasible to check input data for 'credibility'.

(2.8) A typewriter can be fitted to print in OCR B, and this font can be read automatically by optical scanning. What problems would you expect to meet when inputting computer data prepared in this way by an ordinary typist?

(2.9) Give an example of 'data capture at source', and comment on its advantages and disadvantages.

(2.10) Describe the means used to accommodate the very large difference in speed between input data produced by the manual operation of a keyboard and the rate of transfer of data into and out of a computer's main store.

3 · Files and reports

3.1 *Files*

The keeping of scientific and business records is one of
the earliest distinctively human acts. The longest uninter-
rupted set of astronomical observations is still the 400 years
sequence recorded by the Babylonians before the 5th century B.
And, romantic souls were disappointed when the long awaited de-
cipherment of the Minoan script revealed that the tablets from
the palace at Knossos which was destroyed in about 1200 B.C.
recorded nothing more exciting than routine storekeeping. Whe
our records are systematically arranged in an orderly fashion
we have a file; and files are indispensable in any activity
that stretches the capacity and tests the fallibility of human
memory.

It may seem unlikely that enough could be written about
the mere keeping of lists to fill a chapter, but there are man
worthwhile points to raise. Moreover, when files are compiled
on a national scale they contain several millions of records,
their creation and processing consumes a great deal of time an
money, and their design deserves – and gets – the closest attention. Business management and accounts, and government administration, would indeed be quite impracticable on today's
scale and complexity without efficient, accurate and speedy
methods of filing and retrieving information. Whether this is
a boon or a curse is a matter for individual opinion, but the
fact remains, only by improving our methods of storing and re-
calling ever larger volumes of information can we expect to in-

crease the effectiveness and enlarge the scale of commerce, industry and government.

Files are not confined to business men and public servants, they are necessary tools for most professional men and women. Nevertheless, the sheer size of the files kept by national businesses and governments means that these are the ones that present the most severe technical and economic problems; and it is their requirements that determine the designs and set the standards of the filing equipment offered for general sale. In commercial data processing very much more of the data comes from files held in the backing store than enters on any one occasion through the input, and it is essential for this file data to be produced promptly, rapidly and accurately. The data transfer rates of file equipment are, therefore, 100 times or more faster than those of the input peripherals described in chapter 2. Even so, the slower of them may be as much as 100 times slower than the rates at which data move over the main store highway.

The two fundamental questions to be asked about a file are: what should it contain? and, how should it be arranged? The answers depend on:

(a) the nature of the job which the file is to support, and it is fatally easy to take too narrow a view of the uses that will be found for a file;

(b) the operations that have to be performed on its contents;

(c) the technical characteristics of the equipment to be used.

Before we proceed to consider the answers to these questions, as we shall do in par. 3.3, we need to review what peripheral equipment is available for use in the backing store, because its performance affects what it is practicable and economic to do.

3.2 *Backing store equipment and techniques*

3.2.1 *Punched cards.* Early computers used punched cards for holding files, but cards have been completely displaced for this purpose by various kinds of magnetic store. The disadvantages of cards are easy to see:

(a) they are bulky - one reel of magnetic tape can hold as much data as a stack of cards 180 ft (60 m) high;

(b) they are slow - the data transfer rate of magnetic tape is 100 times or more faster;

(c) individual cards can be lost, or a pack can lose its sequence through such everyday mishaps as being dropped on the floor.

The only material now filed in packs of cards is a short program, or a set of constants or parameters to be used with a standard program.

3.2.2 *Magnetic tape.* Computer tape uses essentially the same principles as domestic sound recorders. The tape is a thin plastic ribbon about $\frac{1}{2}$ in. (12 mm) wide, which is coated on one side with a varnish containing oxides of iron. It is wound on reels about 10 in. (250 mm) in diameter which commonly hold up to 2400 ft (800 m) of tape. The reels are driven by electric motors and the tape speed is in the range 100 to 200 in./sec. (2.5 to 5 m/sec.). The coated surface passes under a read/write *head* composed of a set of small electromagnets which replay (read) the data, or record (write) it as rows of magnetized spots across the tape. Typically, one row of nine spots records one byte with an associated check bit, and there are from 100 to 1600 rows/inch (4 to 64 rows/mm). The corresponding data transfer rates range from 10 k to 320 k bytes/sec., and one tape can hold 30 Megabytes or more of data. The method resembles that used for paper tape, except that punched holes can be seen whereas magnetized spots affect none of our senses and we cannot say by simple inspection whether or not a computer tape carries any data; some have found this rather mysterious, but it causes no difficulty in the computer room.

Data are transferred to and from the tape in *blocks* of 500 to 2000 bytes, the tape being stopped between blocks to allow the data to be processed. A few thousandths of a second are required to start and stop a tape, and a blank space must be left between blocks; this *interblock gap* is about $\frac{1}{2}$ to 1 in. long (12 to 25 mm), and it reduces the tape's storage capacity by an amount that depends on the block size; the effective data transfer rate is reduced in the same proportion. Thus, a 1600 byte block recorded at 800 bytes/in. occupies 2 in. of tape, and when it is followed by an interblock gap of $\frac{1}{2}$ in. then 0.5/2.5, or 20%, of the tape is wasted. For a block length of 400 bytes the wastage increases to 50%. However, increasing the block length increases the space that has to be reserved in the main store to receive it, and this space is a costly commodity; accordingly, a compromise is struck between the increased cost of tape and of the time required to run it when blocks are short, and the increased cost of the main store when they are long.

Magnetic tapes are vulnerable to dust, for the particles lift the tape away from the read/write head and cause one or more bytes to be missed or to be imperfect. The tape material is affected by changes in ambient temperature and humidity, and it is largely for these reasons that computer rooms are expensively air-conditioned. The recordings can be destroyed by stray magnetic fields, say from an electric motor, and also by heat; and care is taken to see that *tape libraries* are not exposed to these hazards. It is important to handle tapes with reasonable care to ensure that they are not marked with finger grease, which collects dust, or allowed to unspool on the floor where they may become creased as well as dirty. We have not yet used magnetic tapes for long enough to know whether their records are sufficiently permanent for archives. Moreover, the pace of technical development is so rapid that recording standards change over a relatively short time, and it would be necessary to keep obsolete equipment available to read old tapes. Ordinarily, however, the record is re-copied each time the file is processed, and the question of long shelf life does not arise.

We can protect magnetic tape files against accidental overwriting by means of a *file protection ring* which is inserted into the hub of the tape reel; the ring operates an electrical contact that disables the writing circuits. The records on a magnetic tape can only be accessed serially, and it takes 4 or 5 minutes to read or write one reel of tape, and about another minute to rewind it. Computer tape units are costly items, and the cheaper cassette tapes are being used with mini-computers, but their performance is much inferior, for one cassette can hold only about 500 k bytes of data and reproduce it at about 1200 bytes/sec.

3.2.3 *Exchangeable magnetic disks or disk packs*. The recording medium of a typical exchangeable disk store comprises a 'pack' of eleven metal disks, rather like gramophone records; they have magnetic coatings on their flat surfaces and are mounted together on a vertical spindle with gaps between the disks. The pack is placed on a drive unit which has ten pairs of moveable arms carrying magnetic heads, each of which reads and writes on one of the disk surfaces - the outer surfaces of the top and bottom disks are not used. Each of the 20 recording surfaces is divided into concentric tracks, perhaps 200 of them, and each track is divided into sectors, perhaps 10 in number. The entire pack provides a storage capacity of up to 200 Megabytes, and data are transferred to and from it a sector at a time at data transfer rates of some 800 k bytes/sec. The revolution time is 0.01 sec., and up to an extra 0.03 sec. is needed to move the heads from one track to another. The heads all move together, and it is therefore sensible to dispose the records so that they follow in sequence over corresponding tracks on all 20 surfaces. Such a set of tracks constitutes a 'cylinder', and on average half a revolution, that is 0.005 sec., is needed to reach any sector in such a cylinder.

3.2.4 *Fixed disks and drums*. It is possible for a disk to be fitted with an individual read/write head for each track. A machine of this kind, with several hundreds of heads, is both bulky and expensive, and because its disks do not have to be changed they can be made larger than those of exchangeable disk stores. The tracks are divided into sectors holding one or two kilobytes, and total capacities of 5 to 10 Megabytes are typical. The average access time to *any* sector is about 0.005 sec., and the data transfer rate may approach 3 Megabytes/sec. In an alternative mechanical arrangement the recording surface is disposed round the curved surface of a drum which revolves rapidly under a battery of read/write heads. The merits of drums and fixed disks are lower average access times and faster data transfer rates than those of exchangeable disk stores, but their total storage capacities are lower.

3.2.5 *Optical stores*. None of the magnetic file techniques is wholly satisfactory for really large files, and attempts have been made to develop stores using micro photography. Very large capacities should be possible by using laser light, and lasers would also make it possible to employ holographic methods to protect the store against the loss of data should any part of the recording medium be damaged. Optical stores would be particularly suitable for archival or reference files which needed amendment only rarely, for they are likely to be easier to read than to write. However, magnetic methods have become too well established commercially for anything less than a 'break-through' to displace them, and this has not yet happened.

3.3 *The use of files.*

The simplest way of using a file is to process its record one-by-one in sequence. For example, a payroll file contains separate record for each employee, which is part of the input the pay calculation, and which is itself amended by the result Every employee expects to be paid, so every record is processe the processing is repeated at weekly intervals, and between pr cessings the file is dormant. Such a file may well be held or magnetic tape, for serial access is no disadvantage when every record has to be processed; and the sequence of records in the file can be arranged to suit the circumstances of the job.

Quarterly bills for gas, electricity or telephone service provide another example in which every record is processed at regular intervals. Bank accounts however, need different treatment for the customers of a bank vary considerably in the use they make of their accounts, and it is desirable to be abl to report the credit balance of any account at any time. Processing at long intervals would not be adequate, for the account file needs to be posted with deposits and withdrawals as they occur: for this reason, and for answering credit enquirie quick access is needed to any account in the file. These requirements indicate the use of exchangeable magnetic disks rather than magnetic tape. When the file is too long to be accommodated on the number of disk packs that the computer can mount and keep spinning ready for immediate use, then it is arranged that the more active accounts are kept on the mounted disk packs, with the less active accounts on other packs which can be mounted one at a time on a disk unit which is reserved

46

for this purpose. In this way a reasonably quick service can be offered even for the infrequent enquiry. In some applications the file is a short one, but very quick access is essential: these circumstances indicate the use of a fixed disk. Thus, the next few month's flight plans of an airline may be stored on a fixed disk for use in the reservation of seats; the booking clerks interrogate the file from remote enquiry terminals, and a while-you-wait service is provided to perhaps a hundred separate points from the one central file. Fixed disks may also be used in shared computer services to hold the file of standard software from which programs are called on-demand as users happen to ask for them.

3.4 *File content and organization*

3.4.1 *Content.* What a file needs to contain depends on the nature of the work it is supporting, and on the numbers and types of users allowed to have access to it. There are four common user situations.

(a) Private files

    (i)   Single-user files maintained for the benefit of one person or authority; most of the really large files are of this kind, and many of them hold the data for just one job.

    (ii) *Database* files, which hold data needed for different purposes by a group of related users, for instance, the managers in various departments of a large organization; thus, a file containing data about individual employees and the hours they have worked may provide a base of common data for separate programs dealing with payroll, personnel work, and cost accounting. Databases provide a valuable means of internal communication in a large organization, and greatly assist the coordination of its activities.

(b) Public files

    (i)   Shared files, as when individual users of a common computer service arrange to open the whole or parts of their files to certain other users nominated by them.

    (ii)   *Databank* files, which are databases containing data of a general character, but usually restricted to some context of interest – say, economics or medicine; these files are open to a wide spectrum of individual users.

The contents of multi-user files, including databases and databanks, are protected by controlling the numbers and kinds of users allowed to write in them; for, whereas reading leaves the record unchanged, the addition, deletion or amendment of data affects all subsequent users, and uncontrolled writing in files rapidly engenders chaos. Various technical means are available to protect files; and for reading also it is usual to provide for selective access in which different sets of records and facilities are opened to different users.

Files held in a computer's backing store cannot be as discursive, or as unstructured as some manuscript files, for the medium and its processing are both expensive. This restriction is not too troublesome for commercial files related to accounts, stores, manufacture and sales, for the material in these is customarily terse and relevant; but it poses severe problems of selection and compression for files concerned with human factors, for example, personnel and medical records, which may need to express qualitative judgements and subtle shades of meaning that cannot readily be codified.

With none of the equipment now in use in backing stores is it economical to find and recover a single data word; hence it is usual to deal with *blocks* or *sectors* containing 20 to 50 or more words, which are transferred to and from the backing store as a unit. Again, it is easier to handle a file in which every record has the same, fixed, length; but most jobs generate records of variable length, which means using a fixed length large enough to hold the longest record, thus wasting both recording material and the time needed to pass over the blank spaces in most of the records. Alternatively, we can provide ways of marking and recognising the ends of records, but this makes for more complicated processing

3.4.2 *File organization.* Our word file derives from the Latin filum - a thread, and it is the thread of ideas which runs through a file linking its contents together that distinguishes it from a mere collection of records. The relationship between adjacent records, its system of organization, is the most fundamental property of any file. Consider first, the structural elements of a computer file, and because it is always easier to think in terms of a concrete example, let us take a file of payroll data recorded on magnetic tape. The smallest data element is, of course, an individual bit, but in practice we usually read and write data in entire rows of 8 bits (one byte). A byte may represent one letter or two packed decimal digits. The next higher unit is the *field*, which is a string of bytes that represents one complete item of data; in our payroll file one field of 20 bytes may represent the employees name, and another of one byte only will suffice for sex and marital status. A set of logically related fields makes up a *record*; for example all the payroll data filed for one employee. The next higher formation is the *block* and, as we saw in par. 3.2.2, this is determined by machine requirements and not by any logical relation between the records that happen to be included in it. If the file is a large one, it will extend over several reels of tape, each containing perhaps 5000 blocks.

A record consists of a set of data fields plus a *key* field which identifies and labels the record for the purposes of filing and recovery. The choice of key will depend on the use of the file, and in one record different fields may be used as keys for different purposes. Thus, our payroll records may use 'pay number' as the key for the accounting programs, 'date of birth' for statistical analyses by the personnel department, 'home address' for a transport study, or 'employees name' when we need to print out an alphabetical list. Even so, we have to select one particular key to set the sequence of records in the file – say, ascending order by payroll number – and clearly it will usually be the one that corresponds to the dominant use. This sequence, the relationship between key fields that establishes it, and the sequence of fields within each record, constitute the *file organization*: and the degree of harmony between that organization, the inherent structure of the filed data, and the nature of the work to be done, has a substantial effect on the effectiveness of whatever processes use the file. Any old list is simply not good enough.[1,2]

Sequencing is not always a straightforward matter. Consider, for example, alphabetical order: in dictionaries it presents few problems, but it is more troublesome when arranging a list of names and addresses. What should we do about initials? How do we relate them to those who wish their Christian names to appear in full? How should we deal with the John Smith's? Or, the Macdonalds, the Mac Donalds and the McDonalds? How should foreign names be handled? What about trade names that include, or begin with, numerals?

Much of what is said above about files on magnetic tapes applies also to files on exchangeable magnetic disks. A disk pack has a higher storage capacity (200 Megabytes) than a reel of tape (30 Megabytes) so that fewer of them are needed to hold a large file; and a block on the tape corresponds to a sector on the disk. A more important difference is that it is possible to reach any sector on a disk in less than 0.04 sec., whereas 4 or 5 minutes are needed to reach the last block on a reel of tape. This does not mean, however, that sequencing is unimportant for files held on disks. As we saw in par. 3.2.3, 0.005 sec. is the average access time to records within one track - or one cylinder of corresponding tracks, but when a change of track is necessary a further 0.03 sec. may be required. Hence, when the nature of the task allows us to process the records systematically we can save time by laying them out in sequence within each cylinder, and continuing the sequence smoothly over neighbouring cylinders.

Working files are rarely static, for new records are added, existing ones amended, and old ones deleted; and it may not be easy to do all this without disturbing the location of other entries, especially when the records are of variable length. Sometimes new records are simply tacked onto the end of the file, where they remain as an *overflow* until the next time the file is reorganized. Alternatively, a *random* or *scatter* file may be kept in which the records themselves are in no particular sequence but an appropriately sequenced index is used to indicate where each record is to be found. Or, we may use *chaining*, in which each record contains a *link* that indicates where the next record is located.

3.5 *File creation*

Before a file can be processed it must, of course, be created; and when a major commercial job is first transferred to a computer the creation of its files is a most onerous task, and several programs may be written to assist this specific, once-off, process. The introduction of a computer often brings together work and information from different parts of an organization, and it is almost always found that when the same information has been kept in separate files, say in two departments of the same firm, then the records are not completely in agreement. Errors will have accumulated independently in each and amendments will not have been made with equal zeal. The reconciliation of these contrary data is a tedious task, but often enlightening. The agreed entries are transcribed and checked as input data, and then copied onto the recording medium. The next step is to put them into sequence by sorting them according to the selected key.

A common method is *merge sorting* and magnetic tapes or disks may be used. The unsorted records are first arranged in short strings of sequenced records by a *string generation pass* in which the keys are compared and the records moved as necessary: this process takes place in the main store, and the strings are distributed over 'n' streams in the backing store. An *n-way merge* follows in which records are drawn from the streams to form longer strings, and the process is repeated until the whole file forms one sequenced string. When the file is a very short one, the whole sort can be completed in the main store; and files of medium length can be sorted on magnetic disks by exploiting the fact that a record can be quickly called from any sector. Storage space is at a premium when we are sorting a file in which the records are long ones, but we can detach the records from their keys and tag these with a brief note of where the record is to be found. We can then sort the keys with their tags, and recombine them with the records in a final phase. Sorting has attracted much attention and its extensive literature[3,4] is a standing testimony to the ingenuity of programmers. Unfortunately, no one method is best in all circumstances, for much depends on the equipment available, the size of the file, the length of the records, the sorting key and the amount of order already present in the original data, for this is hardly ever completely random. Programmers no longer need to write their own sorting programs, for the computer manufacturers provide efficient sorting routines as part of their standard software (see chapter 6) and these can be adapted to meet most requirements.

As soon as a file has been created it starts to decay into obsolescence, and has to be kept up to date by additions, deletions and amendments. Indeed, the creation of a large file takes so long that some of its records will be out of date before the process is complete. We can cope with this by accumulating amending data on a *change file* which we use to *update* the master file when it has been completed. Magnetic tape files are updated *serially*, that is, their records are amended in the order in which they appear on the tape. The result is copied into a completely new and up to date file; the old file is not erased or overwritten, indeed it is usually preserved until the updated version has itself been used and found to be acceptable. The old tape is called the *father tape*, the new one is the *son*, and two or three 'generations' of a file may be kept, with their amending data, so that in the event of loss or damage the current file can be regenerated from its father or *grandfather tape* as appropriate. The older generations may be kept in a separate building – a 'disaster store' – in order to guard against fire, flood or sabotage, for the file tapes of a business are a most valuable commercial property.

Magnetic disk files offer direct access to any record and need not be updated serially; they can be processed against unsorted input data, or this data can be sorted and the file updated *sequentially*, that is, in the sequence set by its key fields. The old records of disk files are overwritten rather than copied onto a new file, and as a safeguard against error or mishap it is usual to copy the file and the amending data onto magnetic tapes at regular intervals – perhaps daily; this process is known as 'dumping'.

3.6 *The retrieval of data*

The simplest retrieval of data from a file occurs in response to a straightforward request to locate and print out certain fields of a record bearing a named key, for example, t print from a bank ledger file the current balance recorded under Account No. 78326. It is easy enough to write a *report program* to extract information in this way, and most computer manufacturers supply as part of their standard software a *repo generator (RPG)* which is able to generate automatically an individual report program tailored to meet the requirements specified by a user.

At the other extreme we face the fearful problems of *information retrieval* from a database or databank in response t a rather woolly request from a casual user who may not know p cisely what he wants, nor what records exist or what they con tain, and who did not allocate the keys. His request, or to put it more pompously, his specification of the record's *descriptor* is most unlikely to correspond with the descriptors embodied in the key fields. An attempt may be made to overcome this difficulty by constructing a *thesaurus*, that is, a list of related terms from which any enquirer is required to choose the descriptors he uses. It has also been proposed to allow any element of the record to be treated as a potential descriptor, but this is far from easy for long records. We should not be too surprised that no fully satisfactory system of information retrieval has yet been devised, for the proble of how to classify information for storage so that we will be able to recover it for any of an unlimited and undefinable range of future purposes has plagued librarians for centuries

3.7 *Output equipment and techniques*

3.7.1 *Introduction.* The reports generated by the processing of files issue in the form of visual displays or printed material. Computer output is in many ways simpler than input because it is generated under the programmer's direct control, and thus escapes the variations, errors and ambiguities that accompany the input of data from the outside world. Because we can control it, there is a temptation to be parsimonious when designing output reports; for example, most bank statements are compressed into a cryptic form that conveys little to their anxious readers. Too often the computer is blamed for this, but a computer can be programmed to print as much information as anyone is likely to want, as some banks' statements show. The blame for too fierce a curtailment is probably to be laid at the doors of cost accountants and office efficiency experts engaged in a Scrooge-like saving of their pennies at our expense. The operational messages which computers send to their control consoles also favour the curt and the obscure, and here again there is no inescapable reason why this should be so. The most charitable explanation is that it is mere thoughtlessness on the part of programmers lost in a private world of art and technique. It cannot be denied, however, that it throws a cloak of professional mystique over what is really rather a routine activity, and that is a circumstance which is good for the morale of the computer operator.

3.7.2 *Output displays.* Visual display units (VDU) provide a widely used form of output as well as input, and programs can be written to present the material in whatever format best helps us to absorb its information quickly and accurately. More limited requirements can be served by indicator lamps, or by the electronic types of numerical display, using liquid crystals or light emitting diodes, which are popular in pocket calculators. A spoken output can be provided by combining pre-recorded phrases in the manner made familiar by the telephone system's speaking clock.

3.7.3 *Printed output.* We often require a permanent record (*hard copy*) of a computer's output, either to examine at leisure or to send to others to stimulate them into action – say to cause them to pay a bill. A wide variety of printing mechanisms is available for this purpose.

(a) *Electric typewriters* are relatively slow, printing one character at a time at rates of about 10 char./sec.; the are therefore used where only small amounts of output have to be printed, as for instance the operational mes ages on the control console, or the answers to occasion interrogations of a file.

(b) *Line printer* is the misleading name of the most common form of computer printer, the name is an abbreviation of 'line-at-a-time printer' and has no reference to telecom munication lines or to whether the printer is operated i an 'on-line' or 'off-line' mode, see chapter 5. Most li printers achieve their high speeds by printing *on the fl* that is by aiming well-timed blows at moving type, and a whole line of perhaps 130 to 160 characters is printed i a single machine cycle. In different designs the type i carried on a rotating barrel, on a moving chain, or on the teeth of an oscillating metal comb. A few models print by means of stylus wires which produce a pattern c dots outlining the character. The faster line printers operate at speeds up to 1200 lines/min.; and at this rate the entire Bible, Old and New Testaments, could be printed in 30 minutes. They can also be programmed to skip very rapidly over the blank spaces between lines that are usually left to mark off different items of out put. The paper is fed from a fan-folded stack, and *mult part sets* complete with carbon paper can be used to pro- duce up to 6 copies at one printing.

For business use the paper is usually pre-printed

with headings and other fixed information. The printer room of a large commercial computer is a striking sight, and a very noisy place, and it is served by an array of auxiliary machines - fork lift trucks to move the tons of paper, slitters to trim off the sprocket hole edges, bursters to separate the individual documents from the roll by tearing along the dotted lines, machines to fold and insert them into envelopes, and efficient despatch services to dispose of the results. Computers may one day help to bring about the cashless society, but they show little sign of bringing a paperless one. The fact that fast printing is possible is no reason why it should be done; it is costly, and it wastes time, paper and eff- ort unless the flood of print is actually read.

(c) *Typesetting* is used for hard copy when hundreds of copies of the same output are required. The computer is pro- grammed to produce a magnetic tape that is then used to control an automatic typesetting machine. Telephone dir- ectories are produced in this way by extracting informa- tion from the files that are also used in the calculation of telephone bills.

3.7.4 *Microfilm*. A computer can control a cathode-ray tube that displays characters or diagrams which can be continuously and automatically photographed on microfilm. This is a useful way of producing archival records, and also for generating read- able copies of relatively inactive large files - for instance, library catalogues. Computer output on microfilm can cope with non-Roman alphabets, for instance the Cyrillic, and with non- alphabetic scripts, for instance Chinese characters.

3.7.5 *Output for re-entry*. Mention was made in chapter 2 of turn-round documents printed and despatched to capture data for re-entry to the next run of the file. Updated files on magnetic tapes or exchangeable disks are another form of re-entry output. Tapes and disks may also be used for the exchange of files between different computers, but this can be difficult because problems of compatibility arise even when the two computers are of the same make and model. Obviously, it is necessary for the receiving computer's program to know the file organization used in the incoming material, and also what code has been used to record the data. There is an 'American Standard Code for Information Interchange', (*ASCII*). More troublesome problems can arise at the engineering level, for the adjustments are critical and small differences between installations maintained by different staff can lead to errors or even to being unable to read each others' material.

3.7.6 *Output checking*. Output as well as input needs to be checked for errors. These may arise as a result of undetected errors in the input data, or from mistakes during the processing, or in the course of transfer to the output device. The principles used in checking are similar to those used for input. Check characters monitor all transfers of data within the computer, control totals are used, and an *echo check* from the printer tests that the character it is about to print is the one that was sent to it.

Item and record codes can be checked to see that they are valid. Credibility traps can be set, for instance, that no man on a weekly payroll should receive more than £100 net, or that no quarterly bill should differ from its corresponding predecessor by more than ± 30%. When the traps are sprung, or a check fails, then the item is diverted for human scrutiny and action; but this, too, is fallible and its occasional failures explain some mis-called computer bloomers.

3.7.7 *Graphical output*. The cathode-ray tube screen associated with a light pen (chapter 2) can display computer output in the form of charts and diagrams. For engineering and architectural drawings the computer can be programmed to re-calculate the position of key points in the drawing as they would be seen from different points of view, and by doing this continuously for a series of adjacent positions it is possible to make the represented object appear to rotate. This valuable facility allows the designer to see it 'in the round'. Hard copy diagrams can be produced by various forms of *graph plotter*; one of the most advanced prints with three fine jets of coloured ink - magenta, yellow and cyan - which are controlled electrically. A resolution of 5 lines per mm is obtained, and some 4 Megabits of data can be plotted in less than 2 minutes. The machine is used to produce coloured maps and charts. When the highest precision is required, the computer controls a flat-bed draughting machine which produces full-sized engineering drawings. It is also possible to produce moving cartoon films from a cathode-ray tube display by using the computer to interpolate between key frames in order to animate the result.

3.7.8 *Control output.* In process control, and in traffic control, the computer's principal output consists of electrical signals which operate valves, traffic lights and other regulatory devices. Computers are used also to generate the tapes that drive numerically-controlled machine tools.

3.8 *Bibliography*

The design of files is discussed in chapter 5 of:

(1) *Basic Training in Systems Analysis*, ed. A. Daniels and D. Yeates, Pitman Publishing, 1970.

And in

(2) *Use of Files*, by D.R. Judd, Macdonald, 1973.

Sorting has attracted a great many authors, and a complete
study of its literature would be productive of mental indi-
gestion: two useful accounts, each with bibliographies, are:
(3) *Sorting*, by W.A. Martin, Computing Surveys, Vol.3, No.4,
1971.
And in Volume 2 of this series:
(4) *Information Representation and Manipulation in a Computer*
by E.S. Page and L.B. Wilson, Cambridge University Press, 1973
The characteristics of the backing store equipment used to
hold computer files, and of the printers and visual display
units used for output, change rapidly as technological development proceeds apace and for current information reference
must be made to their manufacturers' literature - but keep
the salt cellar handy.

EXAMPLES 3

(3.1) Compare by examination the alphabetic orders of a dict-
      ionary and a telephone directory. Why do they differ?
      List the rules that appear to have been used in compil-
      ing the directory.

(3.2) Explain how technical limitations of the recording med-
      ium influence the design of a computer file. Compare
      the merits of punched cards and magnetic tape for hold-
      ing:
      (a) a wholesale merchant's file of deliveries - items,
      quantities and prices - to individual customers during
      a preceding month period;
      (b) a scientific program comprising 200 instructions.

(3.3) Compare and contrast the design requirements of files
      for:
      (a) regular business use - as in Question 3.2 (a);
      (b) recording the medical histories of individual pat-
      ients in a national health service.

(3.4) The catalogue of a major library is filed on magnetic tape, and the items listed include publications in all the major languages. Discuss the problems of printing a copy of the catalogue. What alternative to printing could be used to permit a visual check of the contents?

(3.5) Say what makes a computer file a database; and distinguish between a database and a databank.

(3.6) What operating requirements determine whether a computer file should be kept on magnetic tape or on exchangeable magnetic disks? Suggest three examples of files suitable for tapes, and similarly for disks.

(3.7) A computer file can be sub-divided into successively smaller elements either in terms of the logical structure of its contents, or to match the technical characteristics of the equipment used to hold it. List and define each set of elements.

(3.8) The block size used in a magnetic tape file is a compromise; what factors determine the choice?
Compare the efficiency of tape utilization, and the effective data transfer rates for blocks of (a) 1024 bytes, (b) 4096 bytes, when using computer tape recorded at 800 bytes/in., with inter-block gaps of 0.8 in., and operating at a tape speed of 200 ins./sec.

(3.9) Explain what is meant by a 'cylinder' of records on a magnetic disk file, and indicate the reasons for adopting this arrangement.

(3.10) Compare the performance of two alternative designs of computer output printer:
(i) when printing a continuous text, with no blank lines;
(ii) when printing pay-slips each of which contains two lines of print separated by two blank lines, and fol-

lowed by six blank lines to allow for pre-printed
headings and for cutting.

Design 'A' uses an optical technique to print at 3000
lines/min., and the paper moves continuously at a uniform
speed;

Design 'B' prints at 1500 lines/min., and skips over blank
lines at 6000 lines/min.

Repeat comparison (ii)

(iii) when 4 copies of each pay-slip are required.

4 · Analysis and programming

4.1 *Introduction*

The distinguishing mark of computers is their stored program control, for it is its exploitation by the ingenuity of their programmers which gives computers their power. The programmer combines the relatively inflexible unit operations of the machine into sequences of action that achieve an astonishingly wide range of results. There is never just one possible program for a job, the programmer is not looking for a unique solution; hence, there is scope for individuality and flair in programming.

Four stages can be distinguished in the preparation of programs, namely:

(a) Job selection and description, in which the user's task is analysed and defined in a *Job Requirement Specification*;

(b) *Systems Analysis*, which covers the design of a computer system to meet the specified job requirement and its documentation in a detailed *System Definition*;

(c) *Programming*, which encompasses the design of a program that will allow the chosen computer to satisfy the system definition and its documentation in a *Program Specification*;

(d) *Coding*, which covers the writing and testing of instructions to meet the program specification.

Some short scientific and mathematical programs can be written and tested by one person in an hour or two, and for such as these our four stages are telescoped, and the documentation may merely be a printed copy of the final program, for this will be brief enough for anyone to read and understand.

However, the programs for some major commercial applications can total 200,000 or more instructions, and 200 people may work for a year or two on their preparation. In a task of this magnitude it is essential to have completely explicit documentation at each stage to maintain continuity, and to prevent misunderstanding, frustration and waste of time and money. The problems of analysis and programming can indeed be most starkly displayed in terms of commercial data processing, and we shall therefore focus on it; but, first we need to look at the special features of the other two main fields of use, that is, at mathematical or scientific computing, and at automatic control systems.

4.2 *Scientific sums*

In science and mathematics the choice and specification of the job to be done is usually straightforward - some particular calculation is to be made. Nonetheless, it is necessary to specify the range and precision of the input data, the acceptable error level, and the format to be used when presenting the results. The next stage, known as *Numerical Analysis* rather than systems analysis, is to devise a step-by-step arithmetical method of achieving the desired result, for computers are not designed to handle mathematical formulae directly. This restriction to arithmetic is not so cramping as it might seem to be, for numerical methods are available for the solution of most equations and the evaluation of most formulae; moreover, formal mathematics grows ever less competent the nearer we approach the untidy, gritty complexity of the real world. Most practical problems either cannot be solved mathematically - non-linear differential equations, for example, defy formal methods of integration - or they yield functions that are not amenable to the calculation of specific results. The subject is a large one, and it would be foolish to pretend to deal with the methods of numerical analysis here; for details reference should be made to one of the many books on this subject.[1,2,3]

Numerical methods are not exact, but they can be as precise as the situation requires, and an important part of the analysis is the estimation of the errors that arise not as a result of mistakes but from:

(a)   inexact input data, due to measurement or sampling error;

(b)   the use of approximation, as when an infinite series is chopped off after so many terms in order to complete the calculation in a finite time;

(c)   rounding errors arising from the limitation imposed by the computer's word length.

Different calculations are affected differently by these sources of error, and as the mathematician Norbert Wiener said: 'Unless care is exercised in setting a problem up, these (the errors) may completely deprive the solution of any significant figures whatever... the ultrarapid computing machine will certainly not decrease the need for mathematicians with a high level of understanding and technical training.' Mistakes occurring in the calculating process can be checked by repeating the calculation; by calculating and comparing the difference between successive results, or by graphing them; by testing that the result has the expected order of magnitude, and so on.

The result of numerical analysis is to produce an unambiguous list of instructions specifying the sequence of elementary operations which will be used to make the calculation; obviously the number of instructions must not be infinite, and the finite sequence is known as an *algorithm*. Algorithms deal with the general cases, and can be used with any suitable input data. Not every type of calculation can be solved with an algorithm; and not every algorithm is a feasible one, for it may require too much time or too large a computer store.

A common feature of mathematical computing is successive approximation by an *iterative process* in which an initial crude result is gradually refined by repeatedly performing a looped sequence of instructions until successive results differ by less than the acceptable level of error. Consider, for example, Newton's process in which if y_o is an approximate value for the square root of x then

$$y_1 = y_o + \tfrac{1}{2}(x/y_o - y_o) \quad \text{is a better value,}$$
$$y_2 = y_1 + \tfrac{1}{2}(x/y_1 - y_1) \quad \text{is closer still, and so on.}$$

Thus, suppose that x = 36, and that our first guess is $y_o = 4$, then we find that $y_1 = 6.5$, $y_2 = 6.02$, $y_3 = 6$, $y_4 = 6$, and so on. It is easy to verify that the same result is ultimately achieved whatever positive starting value is chosen for y_o. Computers are well suited to perform the mass of tedious arithmetic which iterative processes require.

Scientific programming is not concerned only with devising an algorithm and a corresponding set of instructions. The organization of the work, and of the input and output is at least as important, and quite often more of the program's instructions will be taken up with organization than with arithmetic. Some major scientific programs process large volumes of data in a search for regularities, but a high proportion of them is concerned with relatively short calculations, and the writing of these is an easier task than programming for commercial data processing. First, the scientist generally has a clearer idea of what he wants to do than does the business man. Second, scientific programs are often very much briefer, which makes them easier to test and correct. Third, these programs are usually much more ephemeral, and their whole working lives account for much less computer time, so that it is less important to strive for maximum efficiency in design and coding. This last explains why the use of 'high-level' programming languages developed more quickly on the scientific side even though they were not initially very efficient; there was more to be gained by saving the scientists' time than the computer's. For the same reason floating-point arithmetic has flourished even though it absorbs more computer time than fixed-point computation.

4.3 *Automatic control*

Programming the computer used for automatic control is a task for the engineers who design the entire control system, for the concepts and relations involved are too specialist for a lay programmer to grasp with certainty. In this respect it resembles scientific programming, and differs from commercial data processing. Unlike scientific work, however, control places a high premium on efficiency, in part because the programs are very much longer, and also have longer working lives, but primarily because they have to respond on demand and very rapidly to events as these crop up in the plant, network or traffic flow that is being monitored and controlled.

Most programs contain a number of *routines* which correspond to the main processes, plus sequences of organizing instructions which arrange for these routines to be made available in the proper order, or when the necessary data arise. It is its processing routines that determine the speed and efficiency of a control program, and attention is concentrated on them. They may, for example, be written in *machine code*, that is *hand coded* in the primitive language used to hold instructions in the computer's main store (though not in your actual binary!) rather than written in a high-level programming language: and crucial parts may even be written out in full as straight-line coding. Such programs are, of course, much harder to read, or for others to check. Reliability is also of paramount importance; failures can lead to dramatic

and expensive accidents with enduring effects, including perhaps the loss of life. Control programs, therefore, include
checks that fail safe, and they are designed with parallel
paths that provide alternative ways of exercising the more
important control functions.

As compared with commercial programs, there is much less
emphasis on files, for generally these are used only to record
the log of events. Nor do control programs require amendment
as frequently as do commercial ones which have to respond to
changes in taxation and other fluctuations in the business environment. Indeed, for safety, it is necessary to protect
control programs against casual, accidental, malicious or criminal amendment, and they may therefore be held in read-only
stores. The application and value of computers in automatic
control are considered in chapter 9.

4.4 *Commercial data processing*

4.4.1 *Job selection and description.* The importance of choos-
ing the correct job to do, and of describing it clearly, is
obvious enough, and applies to computing of every kind; but it
is of particular importance in business data processing, for
business men are pragmatists not theorists, and they are *not*
accustomed to thinking of the managing of their firms in terms
of data flows and processes. They may, therefore, see the
computer's function as merely to motorize the work of an existing department in order to drive it faster, with fewer staf
and at lower cost. Nor is it easy for them to decide where to
draw the boundaries around a commercial computer system, short
of the entire firm. A great deal of the dissatisfaction of
business men with their computers has come from inadequate
attention to the choice of job, which has resulted in heavy
expenditure on solving the wrong problem; and also from not
sufficiently foreseeing the need for flexibility, which has

later curtailed their freedom to adapt to new circumstances – computer systems are more efficient, but more rigid, than a roomful of clerks.

The choice of job is not primarily a matter for computer specialists, it is a task for a team which includes:

(a) representatives of those whom we will call the users of the system (the managers of the business);

(b) office efficiency experts, and

(c) an experienced computer systems analyst.

The role of the experts is to help the users to refine and clarify their ideas about what it is they would like the computer to achieve; for only the users can decide the goals to be aimed at. Office efficiency expertise brings to bear the skills of *O & M*, *Organization and Methods* which begin by using Kipling's

> '... six honest serving-men
> They taught me all I knew;
> Their names are What? and Why? and When?
> And How? and Where? and Who?'

A knowledge of precisely what is being done, for what purpose, in what time frame, by what methods, in what places and for what managers, rarely exists in one place before the investigation, for it combines the synoptic sweep of top management's bird's eye view with the fine detail of line managers' worm's eye views. The O & M man is then able to apply his other skills, for example Work Study and Operational Research, in order to develop a new and streamlined set of methods and procedures to achieve the desired result. O & M staff are trained to be tactful, and soon have the users advocating their implanted ideas as if these were their own, as indeed they are – by then.

The systems analyst plays his part in the next stage, which is a *feasibility study* that outlines how a computer could operate the streamlined system, and indicates what size and configuration of machine would be needed, how long it would all take, and what would be the cost and savings compared with the existing arrangement. The object of this study is to secure from the Board of Directors the authority to go ahead, and perhaps also to obtain guidance on certain matters of policy, thus:

(a) Should the computer operate for more than one shift per working day, and more than five days per week? If not, then a larger machine will be required and its higher capital cost will reduce the profitability of the project. However, it would also reduce the erosion of profitability by rising computer staff costs, especially those due to extra payments for shifts worked outside normal office hours. Higher capacity also reduces the risk of strikes, because disputes over shift working are avoided, and it shortens the time needed to recover from any strikes that do occur, or from breakdowns.

(b) How much provision should be made for change and growth? The Board will know its own long-term plans for internal changes, and for the development of the business. Changes will also come from external sources, as for instance, changes in taxation.

(c) When should the trades unions be consulted? The introduction of any new computer system into a business will directly affect many of its employees, and indirectly affect them all. It is something of a shock to a line manager to hear that part of his work is to be transferred to a computer: not only does he fear that he may be made redundant, but he also resents the imputation that some of what he has been doing for years was mere mechanical routine - it disturbs his image of high-grade responsible work, and saps his self-respect. Care and understanding are necessary, with early consultation to give time for adjustment, and also to give the affected staff a lively sense of participation in the planning and design of the new system. Only in this way will they feel that it is a new tool which 'we' want to use, and which will enhance our work, rather than a burden which 'they' are imposing upon us.

Once authorized, the system is described in detail in a *Job Requirement Specification* the terms of which are agreed by the users and by the systems analysts. This specification is then recorded in a formal document: its existence will not stop people from having bright ideas for improvements, but these must be carefully examined and the document amended only for the most cogent of reasons, and with the explicit agreement of all concerned. Once the next stage of systems design is under way, the specification must be frozen and all further changes saved up until after the specified system has been implemented. It was Voltaire who noted that "the better is the enemy of the good", and if change is not controlled then by a kind of insidious accretion the system will grow ever larger in size, and its completion date will recede ever further into the future. Getting a complete and self-consistent statement of the job to be done is often the most difficult part of the whole process of putting commercial work onto a computer. For large projects it is normal to establish arrangements for control by regular reviews to check progress against forecasts, and milestone charts or critical path methods, including PERT, may be used for this purpose.

4.4.2 *Commercial systems analysis.*[4,5] It is the job of the *systems analyst* to convert the Job Requirement Specification into an efficient set of computer processes suitable for a machine of the size and cost authorized as a result of the feasibility study. He examines the sources, volumes and timings of the input data, and makes design decisions about such matters as : the methods of data capture and transmission to the computer centre - or centres; the methods of conversion to machine-readable form - and the nature and extent of the check to be used. Similar considerations apply to the output of results, and it is necessary also to determine the content and layout of visual displays, printed copies, re-entry documents and data, including data to be exchanged with other systems or other computers.

Commercial data processing is above all else a matter of processing files; and the files to be used, their contents, sizes and detailed organizations will all need the most careful consideration: much will depend on whether they are for one job only, or are part of a database. The methods of file protection in particular, will depend on the number of users, or computer processes, permitted to have access to them. The file updating cycle greatly affects the system design, and especially whether the files are to be batch-processed at stated intervals, or processed on-line as amending data happen to arrive. This will determine whether the file medium should be magnetic tapes or disks, and so whether the processing will be serial or sequential - or random.

The processing necessary to transform the input and filed data into the desired output is split into logically independent sections. Each section is then analysed using such techniques as *decision tables* which set out the alternative course of action required to meet the expected range of circumstances and it is usually helpful to display the logic in a *flow chart* (see Fig. 1.2). It is then possible to decide whether the sections can be combined into a single run, or whether equipment limitations force their division into a number of shorter runs In part this will depend on whether or not the process has to share the use of the computer with others. Methods will need to be designed for the control of errors, and these will interest the firm's auditors, who will have their own requirements to be satisfied.

A problem in the design of commercial systems is that systems analysts are highly intelligent young men and women, hence they unavoidably lack business experience. This can lead them to overlook the quirks and carelessnesses and blunders of ordinary people, and so to design systems on the assumption that everything will run like clockwork - even on a wet Monday morning! The solution is to establish and constantly exercise good communications between the users and the analysts: and, to avoid later disappointment, the users must understand very clearly what the computer system will do, and what it will not do, and this is not really possible unless they participate closely in its design, and finally accept that it fully meets the agreed job requirement specification. The completed design is discussed with the chief programmer also in order to satisfy him that it is free from obscurities, ambiguities and gaps, and that it is suited to the programming constraints of the intended machine. The agreed result is formally documented as the *System Definition*, to which no unauthorized amendment is permitted; and this definition document will be frozen as soon as programming begins. There are two other outputs at this stage. The first is a specification of operational characteristics that can be used to select the computer equipment to be acquired. The second is a progress report to top management that highlights any variation from the authorized costs or dates, and any shortfall in meeting the agreed job requirement.

4.4.3 *Commercial systems: programming.* The *programmer's* job is to design, code and test an efficient set of programs that will meet all the requirements expressed in the systems definition, and be suitable for the chosen computer. The first stage of this work, programming proper (that is, program design), shades into systems design, especially when a high level programming language is used. Ideally, it would be possible to eliminate both programming and coding by expressing the systems definition in a flexible high-level language which could then be automatically converted into machine code instructions, or even used to control the computer direct. Even more idealistically, the systems analyst would be eliminated along with the programmer, and the user himself - manager, salesman, accountant, or whatever - would be able to state his requirements in his own professional jargon, and these would be interpreted directly by the computer. Work is in progress towards this goal, but much remains to be done, and in the meantime we have to use a team of professional programmers to produce and test the instructions for us.

The first task is to plan the strategy. A substantial commercial task cannot be accomplished in a single computer run - files have to be created, test data generated and results analysed, and the main process may need to be split to suit the available machine. The complete set of programs for the task is known as a *suite*, and it is the responsibility of the chief programmer to determine how many, and which, runs the suite shall contain; each run will then have its own program. The speed and the storage capacity of the computer will affect this division into runs, and so also will the need to minimize the amount of operator intervention - say, to change tapes or disk-packs. Intervention slows the process, and is one of the reasons why doubling the speed of a computer does not double its throughput - for the speed of the operators is not also doubled. Intervention also opens up the possibility of mistakes. The programs of a suite are linked by the files they share, which hold the data that passes between them.

The next step is to divide the programs into segments or

modules, which are logical units that can be expressed in about 50 to 100 high-level statements. These modules are the basic units which are given to an individual programmer to write and to test. In this way a large task is broken down into comprehensible pieces which less-experienced programmers can handle. Moreover, when the modules are well chosen it is easy to modify a program without upsetting the whole, by re-writing one or more of its modules. The relationship between modules should be kept simple, and a storage area set aside for exchanges of data between modules. Another strategic decision is where to locate the *dump points,* which are places at which a program can be conveniently restarted after an operating mistake or a hardware fault. Most manufacturers' software has a standard *dump and restart routine* that can be used for this purpose. As well as the programs concerned with the main process, the suite will include a number of programs used only in the early stages, for instance, programs to generate data for testing the main programs, programs for checking the test results, and programs for the initial creation of the files.

The chief programmer is concerned with the effective use of his two principal resources - programmers and computer time for testing programs. The first he promotes by allocating modules to individuals, and by using the usual managerial techniques of planning and control to monitor achievement. The second requires the exercise of quality control to protect the computer from trivial programming errors. The programming of a large commercial suite is a major task that can occupy 100 to 200 people for up to 2 years - which produces a bill for their salaries alone of some £500,000 and it is essential to plan the work in detail.

4.4.4 *Commercial systems: coding.* Up to this point not one line of code - one instruction - has been written; but it is foolish to begin before the plan of campaign is complete, for no amount of clever coding can correct errors in strategy.

An important preliminary is the choice of programming language. A computer holds its program in its main store in a binary representation of the basic *machine code* used to express its individual orders. When programming in machine code we have to keep a meticulous running account of the contents of every location in the store in order to make sure that we do not alter, erase or mislay anything that we will need later, and that we do not use the wrong items of data in the computation. This is a tedious task even for painstaking professionals, and today one of the standard high-level programming languages is almost always used instead. The internationally standardized business programming language – *Cobol*, from *Common Business Oriented Language* – is a kind of commercial pidgin English; for instance, we can write in Cobol:

COMPUTE NETPAY EQUALS GROSSPAY LESS INCTAX

Such an expression is called a *statement* rather than an instruction because, before the computer can obey it, it has to be expanded by translating it into a sequence of instructions in machine code. This translation is performed automatically by the computer itself in a separate, preliminary process called *compiling* which runs under the control of a *compiler* program that is part of the manufacturer's software. When expressed in high-level language statements a program is called a *source program*; it is fed as input data to the compiler run and the output is an equivalent *object program* in machine code. A great many high-level languages have been devised, the most widely used are:

Cobol[6] and PL/1[7] for business programming, *Algol*[8] and *Fortran*[9] for mathematics.

The main task of coding now begins as separate teams set to work on the modules and the programs in the suite. In coding, errors of two main kinds may occur. First, we have *logical errors* when the programmer mistakenly instructs the computer to do the wrong thing; say, to add income tax to gross pay instead of deducting it. Such errors are gleefully pointed out by helpful colleagues on reading the program; and reading for checking is very much easier in a high-level language than in machine code. Second, we have *syntactical errors*; programming languages have strict conventions, and it is easy enough to make apparently trivial slips when formulating a statement; say, in Cobol to write the inadmissible NET PAY when NETPAY is meant. Syntactical errors can be detected by careful proof reading, even by someone who does not need to understand the logic of the program; and they are also found, at the cost of some computer time, when the source program is being compiled, for most compilers detect and flag syntactical errors. The errors of both kinds which are found are corrected by rewriting the affected part of the program and recompiling the whole, or by replacing the incorrect instruction in the object program by an unconditional jump into a separate sequence of correct instructions followed by an unconditional jump back; this somewhat messy method is known as a *patching*.

4.4.5 *Commercial systems: program testing and implementation.* When a module has been written and successfully compiled it is necessary to test it thoroughly to see that it does precisely what was intended and nothing more; the method used is to put in test data and compare the partial and final results produced with those predicted. The test may take the form of a *dry run* in which the programmer himself obeys the instructions in the object program and writes down his results: dry running is cheap, effective and productive of deep insight into the operation of the program. A lazier method uses the computer to carry out the test and print its partial and final results for examination and diagnosis. The aim is to test all paths through the module, and the most common combinations of them. The location and correction of errors bears the euphonious name *debugging*, and it can lead to the consumption of much time and black coffee[10]. When all the modules have been tested, instructions are written to link them together to form the complete program, and these are proved by *link testing*, which also throws up any unexpected interactions between the modules. Eventually, the whole program will have been debugged, and so will all the programs in the suite for the job.

In parallel with the later stages of testing some programmers will be engaged in devising the working procedures and drafting the instructions for the computer operators, and for users throughout the business. This work paves the way for the final stages of testing which begin with *parallel running*; this is possible only where a computer is taking over an existing task, and it consists in transferring part of the load to the computer while continuing to perform it in the old way, and comparing the results. Parallel running tests the program with 'live data', and under the actual conditions of operational use; it can reveal unexpected behaviour patterns, and when it is eventually successful it gives the necessary feeling of confidence to all concerned. It also allows the processing time to be determined accurately. Finally, the suite moves into *live running*, the load is built up and the old system is dismantled.

As for the earlier stages, complete, systematic documentation of modules, programs and suites is vitally necessary. Many of the programming team will eventually move on to other work, and it is essential to provide their successors with more information than a bare source or object program can convey. The drive for urgency and economy in commercial work can mean that documentation is scamped or postponed, and the chief programmer needs an iron will to make sure that this dull but most important chore is not neglected.

4.4.6 *Commercial systems: program maintenance.* Good documentation is of particular importance in the work of program maintenance which now begins. *Program maintenance* is a misleading name, for the work includes:

(a) true maintenance, that is, the correction of errors as these are found;

(b) improvements designed to remove inefficiencies in the first version of the program;

(c) the incorporation of requests for changes that have been accumulating since the freezing of the system definition;

(d) amendments to accommodate system or program changes forced by alterations in the external business environment, for example the introduction of Value Added Tax.

Program maintenance must itself be clearly and completely documented, and each item of it must be authorized by a senior user as well as by the chief system analyst and the chief programmer, because to a greater or lesser extent each modification will alter what the approved system will do.

4.5 *Time-sharing systems*

So far, we have been thinking mainly in terms of programs that will run one at a time on a computer which they share with no other work. The same principles apply when several programs run concurrently, as in *time sharing* (see chapter 5), but there are then additional points to watch: for example, the program will not be able to use the whole of the main store at any one time and the method of accommodating several programs may be to require each to be restricted to one or more *partitions* of the store, so that we must check to see that it does not trespass outside its set limits. Again, the time taken to complete a run will depend on the conflict between our program and its bedfellows in their competition for hardware and software facilities; and on their relative priorities. *Real-time* working (see chapter 5) has all the problems of time-sharing plus those caused by the fluctuating incidence of the input data as these happen to arise from the uncoordinated demands of individual users. Only trials can determine the throughput of the system, and realistic full-load, also called *flood* or *saturation*, *tests* are far from easy to mount for they may involve the actual or simulated operation of 100 or more VDU input terminals.

4.6 *Concluding note*

The reasons for giving a rather lengthy account of commercial programming are threefold. First, to indicate that the sheer size of commercial programs makes their preparation a much more daunting task than most scientific programming - eve though they contain only simple arithmetic rather than, say, partial differential equations. A program of 1000 statements is not merely 10 times more difficult than one of 100 statements, for its internal logic is more complex and, as when building a pillar of children's bricks, small errors may inter act to produce substantial and cumulative effects. Second, commercial programs account for a very much larger expenditure of money, computer time, and human effort than do all other kinds put together - currently amounting to several hundreds of millions of pounds each year. This very substantial volume of work has to be systematically planned, and professionally managed and controlled. It is not just a question of a few intelligent people throwing off some bright ideas. Third, the operation of these programs is crucial to the businesses that have entrusted their accounts, sales and manufacturing opera-

tions to the sole care of their computers. Inaccuracy or
inefficiency is not merely a matter of a few incorrect calculations, or a wasted afternoon; it can make the difference
between success and failure in a large enterprise: hence, the
programs must be right, and right for the right job. (See
Appendix 2).

4.7 *Bibliography*

Numerical analysis has an extensive literature which pre-
dates the use of electronic computers. A simple account appears in:

(1) *An Introduction to Computing*, by R. Wooldridge. Oxford
University Press, 1966.

And:

(2) *Numerical Analysis*, by D.R. Hartree. Oxford Clarendon
Press, 2nd edn. 1958 is a classic.

The National Physical Laboratory has produced a useful guide in:

(3) *Modern Computing Methods*. NPL, HMSO 2nd edn. 1961.

Systems analysis is a newer subject, but an introduction to it
is given in:

(4) *Basic Training in Systems Analysis*, by A. Daniels and
D. Yeates. Pitman 1970.

And in:

(5) *Practical Systems Analysis*, by A. Chandor, J. Graham and
R. Williamson. Rupert Hart Davis, 2nd edn. 1972.

There are many texts on the subject of programming, but useful
guides to the four principal high-level languages are:

(6) *A Guide to COBOL Programming*, by D. McCracken. Wiley,
2nd edn. 1970.

(7) *Programming Language/One*, by F. Bates and M.L. Douglas.
Prentice Hall, 1967.

(8) *Basic Algol*, by W.R. Broderick and J.P. Barker. IPC
Electrical and Electronic Press, 1970.

(9) *FORTRAN IV: A Programmed Instruction Approach*, by J.D. Couger and L.E. Shannon. Irwin, 1968.

Debugging is a detective art, and requires a certain amount of flair; but help can be obtained from:

(10) *Program Debugging*, by A.R. Brown and W.A. Sampson. Macdonald, 1973.

EXAMPLES 4

(4.1) In the 16th century Vieta developed the formula

$$\frac{2}{\pi} = \left[\frac{\sqrt{2}}{2} \right] \times \left[\frac{\sqrt{(2 + \sqrt{2})}}{2} \right] \times \left[\frac{\sqrt{(2 + \sqrt{\{2 + \sqrt{2}\})}}}{2} \right] \times \ \dots$$

Write a program to compute and print the value of π when N terms are used on the right hand side of Vieta's formula where the value of N will be read in at run time as input data. Use your program to explore the accuracy of the computed value of π as the value of N is increased.

(4.2) The design of existing high-level programming languages is aimed at different specialist groups of users, for example Cobol for business men and Algol for mathematicians. Discuss the problems that you would expect to meet in attempting to design a universal high-level language.

(4.3) List and justify the documentation required in preparing a suite of programs for a major commercial application. In what respects would a printed copy of the final Cobol program be insufficient?

(4.4) A given compiler program translates statements in Cobol English into computer instructions in a binary code. Compare and contrast what it does with the translation of input data in the form of English text material into binary code.

(4.5) List, and write brief notes on the sources of error in a scientific program.

(4.6) In commercial data processing, outline the roles of: the O & M specialist, the systems analyst, the senior programmer, the coders.

(4.7) Distinguish between logical errors, syntactical errors and transcription (copying) errors in a program; and give an example of each type.

(4.8) Some of the complaints by managers, and by the public, about the use of computers in business arise not because of software errors or hardware faults, but because the system has been misconceived or inadequately designed. Indicate how this may happen, and suggest how it may be prevented.

(4.9) Write brief notes on the following terms in relation to commercial data processing: instruction, statement, module, program, suite.

(4.10) What special problems arise in programming a computer for use in an automatic control system?

5 · Computer system organisation and operation

5.1 *Computer system architecture*

5.1.1 Charles Babbage invented the computer in 1833, but his
ideas had no influence on the design of the first electronic
machines, and it was not until 1946 that a paper was published
which established the Von Neuman style that dominated computer
architecture for many years; indeed, most of today's machines
are still of this type[1]. Computers built in this style have
a single binary arithmetic unit, they hold their programs in
the same store as the data, and they operate under the control
of one program on one stream of data. Since 1946, development
has for the most part improved the bricks without changing the
architecture. Thus, computers have moved from thermionic valves to transistors, to integrated circuits and now to *large
scale integration, LSI,* and main stores have developed from
acoustic delay lines, to magnetic core planes and now to semiconductor arrays. In themselves, these technical details are
of little interest to the user of computers, even though each
has been heralded as introducing a new 'generation' of machine
but, they have been accompanied by substantial increases in
speed and reliability, and reductions in cost and size and pow
consumption[2]. This is not to say that there have been no chan
ges in architecture, as we shall now review[3].

5.1.2 *Input-output*. As computers moved from the scientific
work for which they were designed into commercial work the vol

umes of input and output increased greatly relative to the amount of calculation, and the CPU wasted much of its time waiting for its slow peripherals to disgorge or swallow data. One CPU was clearly able to cope with more peripherals than were needed by one commercial program, and it was arranged for its valuable time to be shared between several programs operating together. Spooling (see chapter 2) was an early form of *time sharing*[4] in which data transfers between input, output and the backing store proceeded concurrently with a main process.

Peripheral units are commonly grouped in clusters of similar devices - card readers, magnetic disk units, line printers or whatever - with a special-purpose controller to regulate the traffic between the cluster and the CPU. These peripheral controllers have gradually come to assume more powers, and in some systems a separate small *satellite computer* is used for the purpose, especially when the data are transmitted over telecommunication channels linking the computer centre to a number of distant terminals. The small machine is referred to as a *front-end computer*, and its function is to relieve the more expensive CPU of such routine chores as control of the communication network, the queueing of messages, the handling of priorities, input data validation, output editing, the control of data transfers between input, output and the backing store, and the handling of straightforward interrogations of files. A rather different use of a satellite computer is to control high-speed input equipment installed at a remote station to allow data and programs to be loaded there, and to print results on a local line printer. This method of working is known as *Remote Job Entry, RJE*.

5.1.3 *On-line, off-line.* Input and output processes can either be carried out under the direct control of the program they serve, or independently. Thus, input data from a VDU may pass

directly into the main store, and take part in the main proces
and answers to enquiries may be returned directly for immediat
display. This way of working is called *on-line* operation. Th
reference is not to a telecommunication line – even though one
may well be used – 'on-line' has the sense of 'on the producti
line'. Alternatively, the VDU may be connected to an independent equipment which records its input data on a magnetic tape
or exchangeable disk for subsequent use in a main process, and
this method of working is called *off-line* operation.

5.1.4 *Storage*. Time sharing and the use of remote terminals a
combined in *multi-access computing (MAC)* systems which may ser
a group of 100 or more independent users remotely. In such a
system each user needs an allocation of space in the main and
backing stores to support his share of CPU time, and a larger
total capacity is required than it is economic to provide in a
core or semiconductor main store. A multi-level storage hier-
archy is therefore used in which the main store is extended by
magnetic drums or fixed disks, and they in turn may be backed
exchangeable disks. The whole is organized and controlled so
that the user sees it as a single-level store. This is achiev
by anticipating the demand for data, and for program segments,
by transferring them from the disks to the main store ahead of
requirement. The unit of data transferred, typically a few
kilobytes, is called a *page*, and the choice of page size balances the need for extra space in the main store when the page
are long, against the time consumed in shuffling a larger number of pages into and out of store when they are short.

In a hierarchical store each working program has its own
allocation, which it can use as if it were the sole occupant o
a computer with a store of that size, and this allocation may
referred to as its *virtual store*; in America – *virtual memory*.
Because a program's virtual store ranges over the entire hier-

archy, it can be substantially larger than the capacity of the main store itself.

Today, some computer systems include more than one high-speed semiconductor store, which enables them to offer a higher total capacity than it is technically convenient to provide in a single unit. Moreover, because the separate stores can operate simultaneously, their combined data transfer rate exceeds that of a single unit. The effective transfer rate can also be increased by designing the store to accept and deliver several words in parallel. In a multi-access system, multiple stores facilitate the segregation of users of different security or priority classes by reserving different units of store for the use of each class.

5.1.5 *Arithmetic and control units.* Successive hardware generations have shown a steady increase in speed, but a fundamental limit is set by the fact that no electric signal can beat the speed of light - 3.10^8 metres/sec., or one nanosecond (10^{-9} sec.) per foot. Hence, to work faster the electronic circuits have to be made smaller, but miniaturization will eventually reach a practical limit, and greater speed will then be possible only by setting several arithmetic units to work in parallel on different parts of one computation. One line of development uses an array of 100 or more simple, fast, processing units.

However, some types of computation may be irreducibly serial, and not susceptible to this attack, and for them the approach is to attempt to increase the speed of serial processing. First, the arithmetic unit is freed from the chores of fetching and carrying the data and instructions for execution and, as we have seen, front-ending and the use of mini-computers as peripheral controllers are examples of how this may be done. Another method employs a modified kind of parallelism in which the execution of a few successive instructions in a program is overlapped, which is possible because programs contain many instructions concerned with the preparation and marshalling of data and instructions, and these can often be executed independently and ahead of the arithmetic and logical operations that immediately precede them. The technique is called *pipelining*, because we can regard the instructions as flowing in sequence through a pipe, and being worked upon simultaneously at two or three points up-stream as well as in the arithmetic unit.

The control unit breaks down each instruction into the series of elementary machine operations involved in executing it; in effect, each instruction is itself a *microprogram*. In most computers this microprogram is fixed once for all and embodied in the wiring of the machine, but some machines have a stored microprogram which can be quickly replaced by another when we wish to change it in order to change the computer's order code. For example, a maintenance microprogram can be used to make it easier for the engineer to trace faults. Or again, a microprogram can be written to make the computer behave like a different model, in order to take over the work of an obsolete machine, or to test programs for a future one. Microprogramming also opens up the possibility of tailoring the order code to fit the characteristics of the work to be done - say scientific or commercial; and even, perhaps, to fit the characteristics of individual high-level languages - say, Algol or Cobol.

5.1.6 *Multiprocessor systems*. A number of the larger computer systems include more than one processor (arithmetic unit plus control unit), two or three main store units and several peripheral controllers linked by a high-speed data highway as shown in Fig. 5.1. In such a *multi-processor system* the main store units also have their separate control units, and they and the

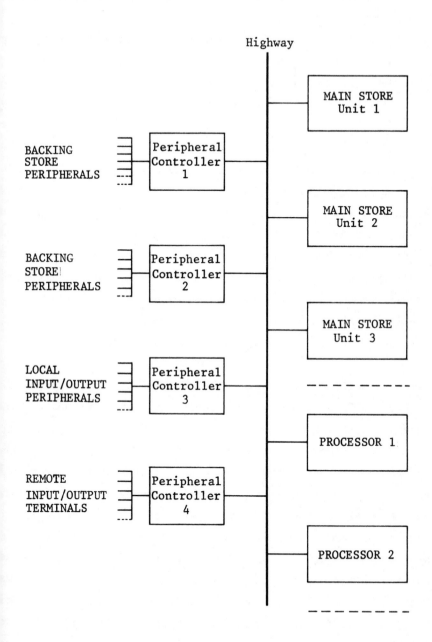

Fig. 5.1   Multiprocessor system

peripheral controllers operate autonomously. The advantages
over arranging the same amount of hardware as, say, two single
processor, single-store computers are:

(a)   greater flexibility in the allocation of storage capacity
      and peripheral units to programs;

(b)   easy sharing of files (databases) between programs;

(c)   greater protection against equipment faults, for the
      failure of any one item does not stop all work, it merely
      reduces the system's throughput - a situation known
      alternatively as *graceful degradation* or working in the
      crippled mode.

Normally the time of each of the processors will be shared between a number of concurrent programs, and the controlling
software enables each to operate without interference from
other programs using the system, apart, of course, from their
mutual competition for resources which causes some delay when
the load is a heavy one. Thus, each program appears to have
its own computer - known as its *virtual machine.*

5.1.7 *Networking.* The components of the multi-processor system
of Fig. 5.1 are located in one centre, but there is no technical
reason why they should not be installed in different locations
linked by telecommunication channels. The obvious way of working is to use these channels to carry streams of bits from one
centre to another and, as in the telephone system, to use switches to make or change connexions as the work requires. This
channel switching becomes less effective when the data messages
are brief, frequent and spasmodic, for the time consumed in
setting up and breaking down the connexion on each becomes too
high an overhead. *Packet switching* is then more suitable; in
this, data messages are made up at their source into fixed-
length strings of bits (packets) headed by a group of address
bits indicating the message's destination. On entering the

telecommunications network the message passes to a switching point, or *node*, equipped with a small computer which after examining the address transmits the packet to the next node in the correct direction, where the packet is stored temporarily while its address is again examined and the next correct route selected; and the process is repeated until the destination is reached. Each nodal computer checks the messages it receives for errors, and requires transmission to be repeated until the message has been received correctly; and they can vary their routing to take account of congestion, or of failures, on the channels connected to them. The whole process may appear to be rather long-winded, but it takes much longer to describe than to do, and end-to-end delays of a few tenths of a second are typical. Packet switching is sometimes called *message switching*, but that term is better reserved for a similar system in which the 'packets' are not of a fixed size but as long as the messages happen to be. Another near synonym is *store-and-forward* working, but that term also covers computer systems in which data messages are accumulated during the working day for transmission at night when the rates are cheaper. Space does not allow a full discussion of the merits of packet and channel switching, and the literature of this rapidly developing subject should be consulted[5].

The close and rapidly growing association of computers and telecommunications is one of the more significant technological phenomena of our time. The hardware and software problems that it poses are as difficult as they are extensive, and their solution will challenge the intellects of computer scientists for many years to come. The result could be to provide us with incomparably the most potent instrument for handling information that men and women have ever had, and one whose use for good or ill could have the most profound consequences for us all.

5.2.1 *Batch processing*. The processing of data a batch at a time was the original way of using computers, and there is a trendy tendency to despise it as somewhat old fashioned, but it remains the most efficient way of exploiting the time of the machine. In many applications the work can be scheduled in advance, there is no need for an instant response, and batch processing fully satisfies the user's requirements; for example, non-urgent scientific work can be processed in daily batches, payrolls in weekly batches, bills in monthly batches, and stock-taking run quarterly.

Scientific work is characterized by small amounts of data and short and relatively unproved programs which may fail; it is therefore desirable to string several separate jobs together to form a single batch, for the changeover time between jobs is comparable with their work times; hence, the faster the computer the less efficiently it is utilized. Commercial work, on the other hand, involves very large volumes of data and the processing time of a batch is usually too long for comfort, for operating mistakes and equipment faults will occur and it is important not to have to go right back to the beginning of, say, a 2-hours batch. It is, therefore, usual to provide break points at intervals corresponding to 10-15 minutes work, at which enough information is stored to allow the process to be backed up to one of these points and restarted when a mishap occurs.

When a large computer is used for commercial work it is normal for its time to be shared between several independent programs each having its own set of autonomously controlled peripherals for producing or absorbing data, and each having a share of the CPU's time.[4] At any instant the computer is executing one instruction from one of the programs, so they run concurrently rather than truly simultaneously. Various sharing methods have been used. In the simplest, the sharing programs are offered in strict rotation equal, brief, allocations or *slots* of processor time, but clearly their moment-to-moment needs will differ and this method is not the most efficient. More complex methods of *multiprogramming* allow the program which is being serviced to complete some specified element of work – irrespective of the time it takes – and there is provision also for the allocation of priorities so that urgent jobs receive more attention and are completed more quickly. When there is a great disparity in priorities the urgent jobs are referred to as the *foreground* work, and the less urgent jobs form a *background* which the computer services when it can. Multiprogramming is most effective when the sharing programs make compatible demands on the system. Thus, two payrolls are not good bedfellows for each requires a lot of processor time for every record on its file, and they would clash continually in their competition for the CPU. On the other hand, when updating a relatively inactive file on magnetic tape, for example a savings bank ledger, most of the time is spent in passing over unwanted records and the demand on the CPU is a light one, so that several such jobs could well share with each other. The number of independent programs running concurrently is known as the *multiprogramming factor*, and by intelligent scheduling we can achieve factors of 4 or more in commercial work. The factor is, however, only a crude metric, for the sharing programs are rarely equal in size or importance.

In straightforward multiprogramming several different programs run together, but it is also possible to run several independent streams of data with a single program, for example, in order to update several separate sections of a very large file at the same time. Because the data streams are independent, at any moment each will be active at a different point

in the program. This raises no new problem if each data stre
has its own separate copy of the program in the store, but th
would be a wasteful way of employing that expensive resource
hence a technique known as *multi-threading* is used to allow
each data stream to thread its own independent way through a
common copy of the program. Multi-threading requires the pro
gram to be written as a series of segments which contain no
references to the particular circumstances of any one of the
data streams, that is each must be a *pure procedure* which
neither modifies itself, nor stores data.

Multiprogramming raises a number of problems. Prioritie
have already been mentioned; next, the sharing programs must
not trespass on each other's part of the main store, or attem
to use a peripheral allocated to another. Thirdly, programs
of different sizes will be being loaded at different times, a
others are completed, and a very flexible method of re-alloca
ting and reorganizing the space in the main store is essentia
and it must be possible for this to proceed 'dynamically', th
is without interrupting the flow of work on programs already
active in the system. These problems are solved by a combination of hardware checking with overall software control b
an *executive* program of the kind discussed in chapter 6.

5.2.2 *Real time operation.* Before digital computers came int
widespread use, analogue machines were used to simulate the b
haviour of complex engineering systems, for example, the elec
ricity grid. When such a simulation proceeded at the same
speed as events in the real system it was imitating, the process was said to take place in *real time*[5]. In digital comput
ing the term is more loosely employed, but it most commonly
denotes a computer system that accepts data about external
events as these occur and produces results quickly enough to
satisfy the needs of some user. In an air-traffic control sy
tem, for instance, the computer must accept data from pilots

radars as fast as it comes in, and process it in time to display results to assist the men who have to take urgent flight control decisions. The essence of real-time working is timely, on-demand, response to externally-generated stimuli. In almost every case the input and output peripherals operate on-line, and the extended term *on-line real time*, *OLRT*, is often used as a synonym; however, to be somewhat pedantic, off-line real time operation would be perfectly practicable provided it met the user's speed requirement.

Real time working is universal in automatic control systems, and it is spreading rapidly into commercial and scientific work. In these latter uses the external stimuli commonly come from VDU's operated by office staff or scientists at their ordinary places of work, and the course of the computer's operation is closely directed by the user's responses to the results which it is presenting to him. There is a kind of dialogue between man and machine: indeed, *conversational mode* or *interactive working* are synonyms for this way of working. The data used, and the choices between alternative routes through the programs employed are moulded by the user to suit his requirements, as these are shaped by the results of the computation. An information system, for example, can guide an enquirer by reacting to his answers to questions designed to concentrate the area of search. Again, by challenging obvious mistakes and testing for credibility an interactive data-vet program can trap most of the errors generated by the unpractised use of keyboards by clerks, scientists and others. And, the computer can reject for immediate correction those silly errors of punctuation and syntax that can waste so much time and mental effort during program testing, and errors of this sort most abound when non-expert users write their occasional programs.

5.2.3 *Multi-access, single-task systems.* In this type of real

time working a multi-access system provides interactive service
to a group of remote terminals, usually VDU's, in support of a
common set of tasks, for instance: airline seat reservation, or
banking. The remote terminals send data to a central computer
for updating or interrogating a central database. The common
tasks are performed by a suite of programs; multiprogramming
is used to share the computer's time between the active termin
als; and multi-threading allows one copy of the suite to serve
many independent users. Essentially, the function of the mult
access system is to improve communications and thus to coordin
ate the operations of remote offices with each other, and with
central headquarters.

5.2.4 *Multi-access, multi-task systems.* Many universities, re
search laboratories and computer bureaux have installed multi-
access systems to provide computing services to some tens or
hundreds of dispersed users operating in conversational mode.
Each user is allocated a virtual machine which he operates as
if he were the sole user of the system. Hardware and software
devices protect users from infringing on each other's allocation of main store and peripheral capacity, or each other's
share of CPU time.

5.2.5 *Disseminated computing systems.* The networking mentione
in par. 5.1.7 can be extended from the dispersal of the components of a multi-processor system to the interconnexion of rea
time systems using quite different makes of computer. The mos
highly developed installation of this kind is the American net
work established by the Advanced Research Projects Agency, *ARP*
which links together a number of computers in universities and
government research centres across the USA. Each main compute
is connected to the network through a small computer of standa
design which serves to match its characteristics - speed, word
length, data representation - to the network, and acts also as

a nodal computer in a packet switching system. Once a minute these local computers check on their own state of health; twice a second they test the data transmission channels directly connected to them; and they send regular reports on these matters to a central network control computer. The aim of the ARPA network is to increase the computing resources available at any terminal of the network.

5.2.6 *Note on real time system design.* Real time system designers are sorely tempted to provide a faster response than the user needs, because it is technically possible and more exciting to do so; however, the cost of a real time system rises steeply as its response time is reduced, for those items that determine this are expensive. In particular, the store must provide rapid access to any item in large program and data files, and the apparatus currently available for this purpose uses magnetic disks and drums, backed by magnetic core or semiconductor stores of much smaller capacity. This two-tier system is clumsy, costly, critical in its air-conditioning requirements, prone to internal congestion and wasteful of computer time - which it uses to shuffle data between its various devices. Hence, economy demands that the speed of a real time system be matched to the carefully established real needs of its users, for example:

(i) the automatic control of air or road traffic, of industrial plant, and of the routing of data messages requires a response time of a few thousandths of a second, because the actions which wait on the response are those of high speed machines.

(ii) seat-reservation systems, in which a booking clerk confronted by a queue of impatient customers requires a response time of about 1 or 2 seconds - not because the customers can afford to wait no longer, but to reassure the harassed clerk that the system is still functioning, and has accepted his request for a booking.

(iii) on-demand information systems, and remote computing facilities, also require a quick initial response to reassure their users but they are then content to wait 10 to 20 seconds for the results; indeed, too rapid a response suggests that the computer has misunderstood the nature of their request and dealt with it at a trivial level.

Computer users and those who sell them systems are also affected by the glamour of real time - none of this imitation stuff! But, real time working is more costly than batch processing for three main reasons. First, much computer time is absorbed in *red tape* or *housekeeping* operations that do not directly advance the computation, but which serve to marshal and control the fluctuating mixture of programs and data and to guard them from each other. Second, the backing store equipment has to be of the more expensive variety in order to obtain the faster performance needed. Third, when users are remote from the computer centre the costs of data transmission links can be substantial. Nevertheless, data transmission and computer costs are both falling, and there are now many circumstances in which remote on-line computing is attractive, and some in which it can be justified.[5] In brief they include:

(a) multi-access systems for scientific computing, engineering design, information services and so on - in which the user gains access to a more powerful machine, more up to date information, or more expert programming facilities than are available to him locally;

(b) computer networks which, as well as offering these advantages of multi-access working, also allow peaks of work to be off-loaded and breakdowns to be covered;

(c)   common database systems used for communication and coord-
      ination within a large organization, or between a group
      of related users;

(d)   applications with an imperative need for current informa-
      tion and quick action, as in industrial automation and
      traffic control;

(e)   applications in which economy or convenience, rather than
      speed, indicate the collection of data from a large number
      of remote points in this way, as in telemetry and domestic
      meter reading.

5.3 *Computer operation*

Accurate and efficient operation of a computer depends on
good order and discipline in the computer room, and the skills
required to achieve this are as much or more those of management as of computer science. Computers are expensive pieces of
equipment, and commercial programs are large investments, and
considerable financial savings can be made by operating the
computer for 3 shifts (5 x 24 hr.) or even 4 shifts (7 x 24 hr.)
per week, but when a system is fully loaded in this way no spare
capacity exists to cover growth or occasional peaks in work, or
to recover quickly from a loss of production caused by hardware
or software faults, or by strike action. Shift working also
makes this last rather more likely because few men or women
like working by night or at weekends, and rota arrangements and
extra payments are a chronic source of friction between staff
and management. It is not enough merely to avoid disputes, the
computer must be operated correctly and effectively if information is not to be lost, items to be missed out of the process,
results to be delayed or to be produced at too high a cost.
Each day's work has to be carefully scheduled to obtain the
highest machine utilization consistent with meeting the performance targets agreed with the users. Operations must be

meticulously logged so that performance can be monitored, cost allocated, and the auditors satisfied that no irregularity has occurred. Magnetic tapes and exchangeable disks have to be checked before use to ensure they are correct for the programs being run, and hold the latest versions of their files.

For batch processing there are two alternative ways of running the computer room. Many scientific installations operate as *open shops* in which any suitably qualified user is offered direct access to the machines, and allowed to operate them himself. This method has the great advantage that users experience for themselves the problems of getting a computer to do what they want it to do; and they are also able to modify and correct their programs on the spot in the light of the results they are obtaining. In this way they acquire at first hand the feel of the controls, and they should be able to write better programs in the future. Open shop operation then, serves the user; but it is not the most efficient way of employing the machine's time.

Closed shop operation is, therefore, more usual in the batch processing of commercial data, where efficiency is important, because the computer is seen as an expensive piece of plant which must be fully exploited, and because the work has to be completed quickly and at the lowest practicable cost. In a closed shop the computer is operated exclusively by trained and experienced staff. Users are not allowed in the computer room when their work is being processed, nor are programmers allowed in when their programs are being tested. Each has to provide comprehensive operating instructions and complete sets of data, and each receives all the results and reports that he needs. The commercial user suffers little from his lack of contact with the machine, for he rarely designs his own systems or writes his own programs. The programmer, rather painfully, benefits from the fact that he is forced to test his programs under the actual working conditions in which they will operate. Moreover, he is compelled to set down in detail all the actions required of the operators in every condition that he can foresee may arise: this necessary chore he otherwise tends to postpone. He is helped also because he will receive a complete printed log of every event and operator intervention during the test run; and this protects him from overlooking actions and decisions which he takes directly, and may well neglect to record, in open shop testing.

So far, we have been considering batch processing, under which the machine rooms of a major commercial installation provide scenes of great activity. The data preparation room is commonly full of keyboard machines with dozens of operators punching and verifying cards, or recording and verifying data on magnetic tape or exchangeable disks. In the computer room itself operators are moving about continually changing tapes or disk packs, loading and emptying punch card or document readers, and tending line printers as these hammer their busy way through piles of stationery. Both rooms are filled with machine noise, and each conveys an impression of congestion, bustle and occasionally, panic. In contrast, the machine room of an on-line centre is uncannily quiet and static, normally very few operators are present, and they tend to be found seated at the control desk engaging in a desultory conversation with the machine through the silent VDU that controls its operation and monitors its load. In large measure these operators are a fire brigade, waiting for something to go wrong; and in future systems even they will vanish and the computer will operate unattended, calling the maintenance engineer when one of its automatic test routines detects an incipient failure, diagnoses the cause and switches the faulty item out of circuit. So far as the computer room is concerned, this will be closed shop operation par excellence, but because the users will have direct access to the system through their VDU's, or other terminals, they will be returned to the immediate contact with the machine's operations that is characteristic of open shop working. In such a system, although efficiency is not unimportant, the user's service and convenience are put first; but as the cost of machine time continues to fall relative to salaries this situation is not as uneconomic as it might at first appear.

5.4 *Bibliography*

An account of the early history of computers is contained in:

(1) *Perspectives on the Computer Revolution*, ed. Z.W. Pylyshyn. Prentice Hall, 1970.

And, the story is brought nearer to the present day in:

(2) *Electronic Computers*, by S.H.H. Hollingdale and G.C. Tootill. Penguin Books, 2nd edn., 1970.

(3) *Computer Structures: Readings and Examples*, ed. C.G. Bell and A. Newell. McGraw Hill, 1971.

However, development proceeds too rapidly for any adequate reference to be given to the current scene, and today's literature has to be consulted. Time sharing is treated in:

(4) *Time Sharing Computer Systems*, by M.V. Wilkes. Elsevier, 2nd edn., 1972.

Packet switching and the need for real time systems are each discussed briefly in:

(5) *Computers, Communications and Society*, by Murray Laver. Oxford University Press, 1975.

And the design of real time systems is described in:

(6) *Design of Real Time Computer Systems*, by James Martin. Prentice Hall, 1969.

Examples 5

(5.1) For machines of comparable size, the speed of commercially available computers has increased by about 200 times, and the cost of performing a unit operation on data has decreased by about 500 times over the last decade.

    (i)   What does this imply for the economic life of (a) hardware? (b) application programs?

    (ii)   Although machine speeds have increased 200 times the throughput for commercial jobs has increased very much less rapidly: suggest reasons for this discrepancy.

(5.2) A computing system may operate with one stream of data or several independent streams, may serve one or several concurrent programs, may have one or several main store and processor units. Tabulate the possible combinations, and comment briefly on each.

(5.3) Computer systems have been variously described as: multi-access, on-line, real time, interactive, and conversational. Define and distinguish where necessary.

(5.4) In comparing alternative computer systems, what factors would you consider, and how would you bring them into a common account, when weighing user convenience against machine utilization.

(5.5) What are the merits (a) to the user, (b) to the programmer, of closed shop operation in the batch processing of commercial work?

(5.6) Say what is meant by microprogramming. Who does it? And, how might it affect the ordinary user of computers?

(5.7) Who would you expect to use a 'virtual store'? In what circumstances?

(5.8) Indicate the connection between the speed of light and the speed of a large scientific computer. How can we surmount the 'light barrier'

    (a)   by computer technology?

    (b)   in other ways?

(5.9) What is the relevance of multi-threading when multi-programming?

(5.10) In the context of data transmission over a telecommunications link, distinguish between:

    (a)   store-and-forward,

    (b)   message switching,

    (c)   packet switching,

    (d)   channel switching.

Which would you use, and why, to transmit:

    (i)   the contents of a large file, say 100 million characters, from one computer centre to another?

    (ii)   messages of a few hundreds of characters each from booking offices to an airline's central seat reservation computer?

    (iii) the daily sales reports from a chain of supermarkets to the company's headquarters computer?

6 · Software

6.1 *Introduction*

Software contrasts with hardware, and is loosely and broadly applied to programs of every kind. Quite often however, as
in this chapter, it is used to denote a set of programs devised
to help the users of one particular make and model of computer.
Software of this kind has generally been supplied by the computer manufacturer, and despite the heavy cost of its production it was for many years supplied free - or, to speak more
realistically, its price was not listed as a separate optional
item, but was hidden in the total bill for an indivisible bun-
dle of hardware and software. Today, software has been *unbun-
dled* for separate sale, and independent software houses now
compete with the manufacturers in supplying it. The earliest
computers had no software beyond an elementary routine which
enabled them to read in data from a specified input peripheral
and store it in specified locations in the main store. This
was enough to allow the computer to read in a program, to which
control could then be transferred. These *initial input routines*
or *loaders*, were usually permanent features of the hardware,
being either recorded in a read-only part of the store or built
in to the wiring of an electronic circuit module. The subsequent development and elaboration of software is the subject of
this chapter.

6.2 *General-purpose programs*
6.2.1 *Subroutines*. It was soon recognized that certain sequences of instructions would be used over and over again, and

that it would be best to write them once only and arrange to make them available for use at any point in any subsequent program. Such a sequence is called a *subroutine*; it is entered by means of a jump instruction in the main program which transfers control to the *entry instruction* of the subroutine. The subroutine also includes an *exit* jump which returns control to the main program. The main program will specify the *entry conditions*, for instance, which store locations hold the operands to be used in the subroutine; and the subroutine contains a *link*, for example an address specified by the exit which determines the location of the next instruction in the main program to be executed. *Open subroutines* are inserted in-line in the main program, and so return control to it at fixed *re-entry points* with no need for a link. In other subroutines the entry conditions determine the point of re-entry, and these are called *closed subroutines*.

A collection of standard subroutines, for example, those for the control of input and output peripherals, or the calculation of mathematical functions, forms part of the manufacturer's software library. In use, the action to be taken is adapted to the particular requirement by parameters specified in the main program. Other subroutines may be peculiar to a user's program and written by him solely for inclusion in it. In either case the objects are:

(a) to make programming quicker by incorporating ready-made routines of proved correctness;

(b) to improve processing efficiency by using routines which have been designed with more skill and greater care than the average programmer can bring to bear;

(c) to save space in the main store by holding a repeated part of the program once only.

Clearly it is possible to use one subroutine in the course of executing another, in such a case the subroutine that is entered from the main program and which returns control to it, is called *first level*, or *first order*, and the subsidiary one is a *second level*, or *second order*, routine. As with fleas, the process can be extended ad infinitum.

6.2.2 *Utility and service routines.* The terms *utility*, or *service*, *routine* are rarely used with much precision. Most often their meanings overlap, but there is something of a tendency to use utility routine for standard programs designed to operate on files, and service routine to indicate those designed to assist the preparation and testing of programs, and the diagnosis of hardware faults.

File management utilities handle general-purpose operations on files, rather than the processing of their particular contents. Typical utilities cover: the creation, amendment, transcription and rearrangement of files, restart and recovery procedures, data retrieval and reporting. Thus, transcription may be performed to copy data from a slower to a faster medium, and can be combined with data vetting, sorting, and merging; or it may be used to prepare a copy of a magnetic disk file by dumping it onto magnetic tape as a precaution against accidental loss or damage. For tape files in particular, there are standard routines to handle the variety of housekeeping chores which arise at the end of a tape; such as checking control totals and record counts, rewinding, and the opening of continuation reels. Again, opening a tape file involves reading data from its *header label*, for instance, the file name, its reel and generation numbers, and its re-processing and expiry dates, all of which are then checked against details recorded in the program or entered by the operator.

Some software integrates a range of utility programs into

a coherent *file management system* covering all of the general aspects of file handling. Where the file is organized as a database the software becomes a *database management system*, *DBMS*, and the usual file utilities are then supplemented by others which provide for various levels of file security, and for privacy between authorized users, allowing each to define his own *virtual files* within the common database by selecting which items and which key fields he will employ. DBMS is a most fashionable subject, and rather too much is expected of what is at present an infant art.

Service routines include the programs used to translate high-level programming languages (see 6.3.4., below) into machine code, and also routines designed to assist the finding of errors in programs, and faults in the hardware. Offline, or *hands off*, debugging is assisted by service routines which can produce printed copies - *dumps* - of the contents of the principal registers in the CPU, and of specified locations in the main store, for the programmer to examine at leisure. *Trace routines* can print copies of the current instructions and operands at predetermined points in the execution of a program under test. It is now possible to test programs online and interactive, *hands on*, debugging routines commonly allow a programmer using a VDU to stop the execution of his program in order to examine the operands or instructions, to relocate it in store, to delete, amend or add instructions, and to print a copy of the amended program.

Hardware maintenance support is given by diagnostic routines designed to exercise every function of isolated parts of the electronics, and to produce results which indicate whether they are working well, and when they are not which unit is faulty. It is not easy to locate faults precisely when using the normal order code of the machine, for after all this was not designed for that purpose but to promote efficiency in programming and operation. In some machines, therefore, the engineers use a separate microprogram that provides an order code more suitable for their diagnostic tests.

6.2.3 *Generators*. We have noted above that programmers no longer need to write their own sorting programs. The manufacturers standard software will include a *sort generator* routine which when supplied with input data specifying the particulars of the application – for instance, the number of records, their length, the nature and size of the sorting key – will produce a version of its standard sort program tailored to the specific requirement. Similarly, a *report generator* can be used to generate an individual version of a standard report program for listing and tabulating data extracted from a file, when it is given specifications of the file organization, and of the format and content of the required report.

6.3 *Programming languages*

6.3.1 *Machine language*. The instructions which a computer's control unit actually decodes and causes to be executed are a binary representation of the order code of the machine. The term *machine language*, or *machine code*, however, indicates not this binary form but its decimal and alphabetic equivalent which programmers use on the increasingly rare occasions when they need to write down instructions in their most basic form. For example, 01 4679 might be a machine language instruction to perform function 01, say add, with whatever operand happens to be held in Location 4679 of the main store. Programming in machine language is a tedious and exacting task for meticulous professionals, for it requires a fluent familiarity with the list of arbitrary operation codes, and the keeping of a painstaking account of the contents of every relevant location in the store before and after each step in the program. Machine language programs are sad stuff to read, and it is very difficult to understand and check someone else's program when it is at all long. Hence, as soon as computers began to emerge from mathematical laboratories various ways were devised to make programming easier.

6.3.2 *Autocodes and assembly languages.* The first step towards simplifying the programmer's task was to transfer the thankless chore of checking and allocating addresses to the computer by using letters to refer to operands, as in algebra. The operation codes comprised the ordinary arithmetic symbols (=, +, -, x, ÷) and the instruction repertoire was extended by using other mnemonic codes to call in subroutines for evaluating standard mathematical functions; for instance, SIN X would automatically call in a subroutine to evaluate the sine of an angle of X radians. A programming language of this kind is called an *autocode*, and made it possible to write in a close approximation to the ordinary 'language' of algebra.

However, a program in autocode cannot be obeyed by the computer until it has been translated into its machine language equivalent - more strictly, into one of its machine language equivalents, for there are many. For this purpose the autocode program, known as the *source program*, is fed as data into the computer and is processed by an *assembler* program which converts the arithmetic symbols and mnemonic codes, assigns addresses, and calls in subroutines as required, and which produces as its output an equivalent *object program* in machine language. The autocode principle was later extended by enlarging its range of mnemonic operation codes in order to make it more useful for commercial data processing, and it is then commonly known as *assembly language*. Usually, the computer used for assembly is the one that will run the object program, but this is not necessary, for an assembler could be written for any machine to convert from any specified autocode into any specified machine language.

The preliminary stage of assembly can be avoided by using an *interpreter* program which converts each instruction in the source program as it falls due to be obeyed. Interpretation is quicker and cheaper when a program is brief, and is to be used only a few times; but it wastes machine time for programs in repeated use.

An autocode or assembly language instruction in a source program advances the computation by only a short step. Programs in these languages are, therefore, not much briefer than machine language programs, but they are very much easier to write, read and check, especially by those of us who are not full-time programmers. These languages have, however, now been largely displaced by more advanced programming languages, and are no longer used to any great extent.

6.3.3 *Macros.* The term *macro-instruction*, invariably abbreviated to *macro*, is used to indicate an instruction in a source program that generates several machine language instructions in the object program. In this it resembles an open subroutine, and the principal difference is that because macros tend to correspond to rather short subroutines they are translated and incorporated in the main program by a *macro assembler* routine before the program is loaded rather than being pulled in during execution, as is a subroutine.

6.3.4 *High-level programming languages*[1,2,3,4,5,6]. Autocodes, assembly languages and macros are usually restricted to particular makes or models of computer, but the programming languages most widely used today were intended to be suitable for use with any machine. Again, each of their instructions corresponds to a rather elementary step, and thus does not allow the programmer to stand back from the mechanics of the computation: in contrast, each source program *statement* in one of today's *high-level programming languages* initiates a longer sequence of processing by the object program. Moreover, the most widely used high-level languages have been designed to suit the procedure commonly used in solving some particular group of problems - mathematical, control system, or commercial. For this reason they are called *procedure-oriented languages*: the obvious abbreviation *POL* serves also for the related term *problem-oriented language*, which denotes one designed for convenience in solving a class of problems, irrespective of the procedures employed. The distinction between these terms is too nice a one for everyday purposes, hence they are used interchangeably and their shared abbreviation gives rise to no ambiguity in practice. The best known POL's are Fortran and Algol for mathematics, and Cobol for commercial data processing: their unattractive names derive from computer people's curious addiction to acronyms.

The use of these languages allows the source program to be written in terms that approximate to those in general use in the subject. Each step in the computation is specified by a *statement* (this term is used rather than instruction to avoid confusion with the more numerous steps of the object program). Algol and Fortran statements, for example, resemble algebraic expressions; in Fortran:

$$A = Y**2 + 4*Z**3$$

and in Algol:

$$a:= y \uparrow 2 + 4*z \uparrow 3 ;$$

will generate object routines to evaluate the expression

$$a = y^2 + 4z^3$$

And in Cobol it is possible to write statements in a kind of basic business English, for instance:

$$\text{COMPUTE NETPAY EQUALS GROSSPAY LESS TAX}$$

The high-level source program is converted into a machine language object program by processing it under the control of a *compiler* program which is part of the standard software. The compiler translates each statement into an equivalent set of machine language instructions, incorporates any standard subroutines required and links the parts of the program together. It also detects and comments on syntactical errors made by the programmer, although it clearly cannot otherwise restrict what he may choose to write. When the source program is a long one, and especially if it is to be used repeatedly, then it will be compiled as a separate preliminary process; but short scientific programs may be compiled and run in a single *load and go* operation, and in this case the object program is never put out and stored for future use.

Each different make of computer requires its own version of the compiler, although different models in one manufacturer's family may be able to use the same compiler. A given source program can be translated and run on any type of machine for which a suitable compiler is available. However, different compilers have different capabilities. For example, the Fortran compiler for a small machine may be a cut down version that does not cover all of the options available in standard Fortran, but only a subset of them – thus imposing restrictions on the programmer, and limiting the range of existing Fortran programs that can be compiled. Again, some compiler writers have provided extra, and occasionally idiosyncratic, facilities not included in the standard language. In each of these ways 'dialects' of the language arise, and more than a hundred dialects of Fortran alone are in use in the United Kingdom. All of the main languages have dialects, and many hundreds of quite different programming languages have been invented. Clearly, the Tower of Babel is a recurrent phenomenon. We may well wonder at the extent of this narcissistic activity, and note that, as in other branches of science, it is easy to be seduced by the beauty of the technique into forgetting to apply it to the re problems which it was intended to solve – not every HiFi enth siast likes music.

It will be apparent that it is far from easy to compare the merits of different high-level languages, for we need to ask: for what kind of problem? what type of programmer? using which compilers? and on which machines? Compiling absorbs ex pensive computer time, and must be as efficient as possible, but shortening the compiling time may not produce the most ef icient object programs, and since these are run repeatedly while compiling is performed once only it is run time effici- ency that is often the more important.

It would no doubt be very nice if it were possible to have a universal high-level language suitable for all classes of problem and all types of processing, and available for use on all current machines; and attempts have been made to desig one. Thus, IBM produced PL/1 which combines features of For- tran, Algol and Cobol; but its critics argue that it is a con flation rather than a synthesis, which has made it clumsy to use and inefficient to compile when it is being used for any one specialist purpose. A Swiss Army knife can perform many functions, but none as well as a tool designed for that purpo Nor have we found any one language satisfactory for all the purposes of human communication and problem solving.

6.4 *Control software*

A large computer is too complex a machine for its opera- tors to direct in detail, nor are their responses fast enough to keep up with the rapidly changing circumstances which aris Hence, it is usual to hand over the moment-to-moment directio of operations to an auxiliary program which is variously know as an *executive* or *control program*, or as a *supervisor* or *mon.*

114

This program includes a number of routines to control the input
and output of data (including the management of a data network),
to monitor the state of all the peripherals, and to regulate
their requests to interrupt the flow of other operations through
the CPU, and to provide for dumping and restarting when failures
occur. The executive also handles the exchange of messages with
the console operators, and does so in a helpful *system control
language*; it logs all significant activities and events, and in
a multiprogramming system it supervises the transfer of control
between users' programs running concurrently, and manages the
allocation of the main store between the different programs.
Some store management strategies do not require contiguous locations for a program but when a program has run to completion,
the executive commonly rearranges the store allocations to the
remaining programs in order to create large areas of contiguous
locations.

The executive program has, of course, to be resident in the
main store, and thus it occupies very valuable space. Its operations share the time of the CPU with other programs active in
the machine, and it has priority over them, and thus it consumes
very valuable processing time. It is, therefore, an overhead of
some significance, and the benefits of extra facilities in the
executive have to be weighed against this overhead cost. For
economy, an executive program is designed for a particular mode
of operation, and a computer may have a number of alternative
executives, say for batch mode (with magnetic tapes, or with
magnetic disks), for multiprogramming, for multi-access, and for
real-time.

However, when the computer system is a very large one it
may be executing many programs concurrently in a variety of
different programming languages, some in batch mode, some using
interactive multi-access, some transaction processing, and so
on. Such a system needs a set of executive routines and compilers able to handle all permissible situations. This set,

together with additional software constitutes an *operating system*[7],[8],[9] which, as well as performing the executive functions noted above, helps the operator to plan and schedule the efficient loading of the computer, to keep detailed operating statistics about the utilization of the peripherals and the CPU, which will be used for charging, and for fine tuning of the load, of the system's configuration and of the operating system itself. In such a system the user does not 'see' the actual hardware; he is confronted by a software facade and see only a subset of the whole, namely, the virtual machine which the operating system has defined for him. Which actual locations serve him in the main and backing stores he neither knows nor cares, unless something goes wrong and this information is automatically printed out to assist his diagnosis. A crucial point is the degree to which such an operating system succeeds in insulating the sharing user programs from each other in order to protect their privacy and preserve the security of their files.

Clearly, an operating system, being a multi-mode executiv with other trimmings, must represent a substantial overhead on the computer's operations. It will be justified, therefore, only where the nature of the work to be done is inherently fluctuating, varied and urgent, so that it is not feasible to schedule a series of coherent phases in each of which a simple and more efficient executive can be used. Again, the same total work load might be carried more effectively by a number of separate smaller machines when it is not essential to share files across the board, or to have the larger power of a bigge machine available for anyone to use. However, computer system are not invariably planned in that cold blooded way, and it is undeniably exciting and impressive both to design and to use a big multi-purpose thumper.

6.5 *Program packages*

Macros, sub-routines and generators all rest on the idea
that standard chunks of computation will recur in many programs,
and might as well be written once for all to use. The same
principle is carried a step further in program packages. These
offer standard methods of dealing with larger pieces of processing. Thus, every firm has to pay wages, and time and money
are wasted when each prepares its own program to apply the same
procedures to achieve the same results. Hence, a standard
'payroll package' is produced by a software house, and offered
for use by anyone who is willing and able to adapt his office
procedures to its broad requirements. Sales control is another
popular area for commercial program packages, and a typical
sales package might cover:

- Maintenance of a sales ledger
- Production of invoices
- Periodic statements of account to customers
- Credit control reports
- Listings of debtors by the age of the debt
- On-demand reports on customer records, discounts,
  catalogues and pricing.

The advantages of using a package are that it:

(a) requires no programming effort, and its development cost
     is shared between all who use it;

(b) is available for immediate use;

(c) is efficient, free from error and proved in use;

(d) can easily be adjusted to match the dimensions of a user's
     work.

The principal disadvantage of a program package is that its
users have to adopt the methods embodied in it, and the input
and output procedures that flow from them. This requirement
sometimes triggers the well-known *NIH*, not-invented-here, reaction in those who cannot bring themselves to accept that an

117

outsider may be able to match or better them in devising ways
to do their work. Sometimes, of course, a standard package may
really be unsuitable, for in the interests of generality they
often adopt the more straightforward methods, and these may be
inadequate in the particular circumstances of some users, especially those in large organizations, which tend to be rather
set in their ways.

As well as payroll and sales, commercial packages cover
stock control, ordering, production planning, financial contro
and modelling. There are applied mathematics packages for
forecasting, linear programming, general statistical work and
simulation studies. There are numerous engineering design
packages, including those for use with numerically controlled
machine tools. Packages have been written for the justification of type, for text editing, for information retrieval and
for scientific calculations, and the list grows longer every
day.

Certainly, packages can be criticised as crude ready-made
solutions, but this need not imply that they are poor fits, fo
when they are written in a modular form and in a high-level
language there is scope for tailoring them more closely to
match special requirements. However, a user needs to be very
sure that the cost of doing so, and even more of writing his
own program where a package exists, will be justified by the
additional benefits obtained - hurt pride is not a sufficient
reason.

6.6 *Software-hardware*

Whatever can be done by software can be done by hardware
and nearly vice versa. At the level of a full-scale commercia
program of several thousands of Cobol statements this comment
is of theoretical interest only. But, for less complex proces
ses the economic balance between hardware and software is tend

ing to tip in the former's favour. The design and production
of software is heavily labour-intensive, programmer's salaries
have risen considerably, and continue to rise, whereas integrated circuit and LSI techniques are driving down the costs
of computer electronics at a rapid rate. The outcome could be
a swing towards hardware and away from software for such things
as macros, sub-routines and some operating system functions.
As well as cost savings, the provision of extra electronics
would relieve the CPU of housekeeping chores; moreover, these
could also be completed more quickly by proceeding in parallel
with the main stream of processing. We have much to learn, also, about the full exploitation of microprogramming in a period
of cheapening electronics. Alternative microprograms might be
used to present order codes specialized to suit particular
types of work, or particular high-level languages. The use of
one all-purpose code is a blunt instrument.

Microprogramming may have a valuable contribution to make
in the conversion of large suites of programs from an obsolete machine to its successor. This is an especially troublesome and costly, but recurrent, activity in commercial data
processing where program suites run to many tens of thousands
of instructions, and represent a large investment of time and
money. Manufacturers already provide software which allows a
new computer to simulate its predecessor: and, in some instances
temporary modifications have been made to the new hardware in
order to allow it to 'emulate' the old machine. Both *simulation*
and *emulation* were designed as temporary expedients to help
users through their changeover crises, and to give them the time
to convert the existing programs 'at leisure'. Unfortunately,
leisure is a scarce commodity in commercial work, and there have
been cases of the third generation machine emulating the second
generation simulating the first generation performing an ancient,
and by now much patched, program whose documentation has never
been kept up to date. At each transitional stage the cry

has been: 'Don't touch it, it works'. Few users of these expedients dare to calculate the efficiency of using the new
machine, or to revise the economic analysis that justified it
acquisition.

6.7 *The growth of software*

Figures have been produced for the total number of mach:
language instructions in the software which one of the large:
manufacturers has provided with his current range of compute:
In 1954 there were 5,000 such instructions; but in 1969 about
5 millions, which corresponds to geometric growth at almost
60% per annum. The design, validation, documentation, distr:
bution and maintenance of so massive a bulk of software is a
large and vastly expensive enterprise. Five million instructions represents about 1000 man-years of work, and some mill
of pounds in cost. Nor is it to be expected that a product c
this size and complexity will be completely free from error.
Unfortunately we are not yet able to prove that a program is
without error, nor is it practicable or economic to test eve:
possible path through a large program; all that we can do is
test it as systematically and intelligently as possible, and
then gain confidence in it in use.

The manufacturer's costs are large, but they are only a
fraction of the total sum involved in the production and test
ing of programs. The larger part of this is spent by users :
developing and maintaining their own application programs. I
tailed statistics are not available, but in the United Kingd
the current expenditure on computer hardware is about £300 m:
lions a year, and a user's costs divide about equally betwee:
hardware, software and operating; hence, about another £300
millions is being spent by users on programming. Software i:
now big business. It is also a business producing a distinc
odd kind of goods, for a computer program is not a patentabl:
invention, nor is it a material product − it is a set of dee:

frozen ideas. It most closely resembles a piece of music, which can itself be regarded as a program for the control of a group of instruments; and, perhaps, the most appropriate way to protect a programmer's work against pirating would be through the recognition of performing rights, under which he would be paid a royalty each time his program was run. However, the policing that would be needed to detect and penalize unauthorized use would involve a great deal of organization and cost.

6.8 *Bibliography*

The art of software is developing so rapidly that much of its literature falls between the stools of unspecific generality or obsolete detail. Programming languages are discussed in:

(1) *Computer Languages*, by P.C. Sanderson. Butterworths, 1970.

(2) *An Introduction to the Study of Programming Languages*, by D.W. Barron. Cambridge University Press, 1976.

Descriptions of some of the more common high-level languages appear in:

(3) *Basic Algol*, by W.R. Broderick and J.P. Barker. I.P.C. Press, 1970.

(4) *A Guide to Cobol Programming*, by D. McCracken. Wiley, 2nd edn. 1970.

(5) *Fortran IV. A Programmed Instruction Approach*, by J.D. Couger and L.E. Shannon. Irwin, 1968.

(6) *Programming Language/One*, by F. Bates and M.L. Douglas. Prentice Hall, 1967.

Control software is the subject of:

(7) *Executive Programs and Operating Systems*, ed. G. Cuttle and P.B. Robinson. Macdonald/Elsevier, 1970.

(8) *Computer Operating Systems*, by D.W. Barron. Chapman and Hall, 1971.

(9) *Operating Systems*, by S.E. Madnick and J.J. Donavan. McGraw Hill, 1974.

For details of the facilities offered by the operating systems of current models of computers reference must be made to their maker's literature.

Examples 6

(6.1) Discuss, from a computer user's point of view, the pros and cons of unbundling software. What consequences do you consider unbundling may have:

    (a)   on the choice of order code for a new machine?

    (b)   on the standardization of programming languages?

(6.2) When a computer is being operated in multiprogramming mode it is useful to be able to hold only one copy of each library subroutine in the computer's store, and to make it available for use by all of the programs which are sharing the time of the machine. What problems do you foresee could arise? And, how may they be avoided?

(6.3) Discuss the difference between a Procedure-oriented language and a Problem-oriented language with specific reference to an application area of your choice, for instance medicine.

(6.4) Why in Fortran do we write:

$$A = Y**2 + 4*Z**3$$

rather than the more usual: $a = y^2 + 4z^3$

And, in Cobol:

$$\text{COMPUTE NETPAY EQUALS} \ldots\ldots\ldots$$

instead of the more natural: Compute net pay equals...?

(6.5) What is meant by a second-level sub-routine? Give an example. How does such a sub-routine differ from a macro instruction?

(6.6) List the facilities provided by a Database Management System.

(6.7) Give the meanings of:

    (a)   generator,

    (b)   interpreter,

    (c)   compiler,

    (d)   a dialect of Fortran.

(6.8) What is the 'Operating System' of a computer? Discover, by reference to the sales literature, what varieties of operating systems are offered by one of the large computer manufacturers.

(6.9) The increase in software provided by manufacturers has been rapid and continuous: what factors may check its future growth?

(6.10) A manufacturer provides effective software enabling his new range of computers to simulate his old range: this clearly offers advantages to users, but what are the disadvantages?

7 · Powers and limitations

7.1 *Powers*

The fantastic powers of computers have been written up
quite sickeningly in the popular press, and extolled in the
sales blurb of their manufacturers. It is, nonetheless, wortl
reviewing why they are so significant an invention. We have
touched already on the breadth of application which their
stored-program control allows; while noting that the resultin,
range and subtlety of their behaviour should properly be cred-
ited to the patient ingenuity of their programmers rather tha1
to any action of the machines themselves.

An obvious source of a computer's power is its great ari
metic speed, for with addition times of much less than a micr
second they can perform as much raw arithmetic in a second as
could a man in his entire 40 years of working life. To put t
gee-whiz statistic another way, one such machine could out-
perform the population of the United Kingdom. Moreover, the
cost of computer calculation is clearly many thousands of tim
less than that of human arithmetic, and the probability of
error is negligible. This comparison is, of course, most mis
leading because it neglects the vital fact that men manipulat
data in much larger steps than the tiny unit operations of co
puters; but even so, a very handsome margin of advantage remains with the machine.

This means that we can now calculate where once we had t
speculate. And, we can afford to repeat quite massive calcul
tions with different sets of data in order to explore a range

of alternatives and select the best. Or, we can do so to test whether our results depend critically on some item of data, and this is especially important when we cannot control that item, or have no way of measuring it accurately: it is useful also when we want to discover whether that item is a significant variable in our equations. These *sensitivity analyses* are particularly useful in economics. Again, when studying complex systems we often find it more practical to simulate the system's behaviour by devising a simplified model of it, than to seek a rigorous analytical solution. Computers' power of handling large volumes of data fit them admirably to modelling and simulation work.

We can easily find ourselves overwhelmed by too rapid a rate of data input when using such products of our own ingenuity as a jet aircraft. Presumably, our brains have evolved to cope with the data flows generated by the responses of our unaided senses to events that occur within eyeshot and earshot when we are travelling no faster than our legs can carry us: it is not surprising that they saturate when immersed in the torrents of data that flow from supersonic flight and global telecommunications. Computers can help by using their high-speed processing to pre-digest the data, to control the immediate reflex actions, and to refer to us only the broad long-term direction of affairs and the choice of goals. As well as being overloaded by too fast a pace of events, we can easily overlook changes that occur too slowly. Here also, we can use computers to elucidate slow trends from a greater aggregation of historic data than we could ever handle alone.

7.2 *Limitations*

7.2.1 *Limitations of current practice.* Today's computers are necessarily limited by today's technology, but rapid improvements in both electronics and in software are continually enlarging the area of the practicable. Major computer systems remain large and expensive, heavy consumers of energy, and demanding in their requirements for air-conditioning, and these unattractive characteristics limit their use; most obviously, where cost and portability are important. Again, fast as they are, it is still rather easy to run out of steam when faced with the appalling complexity of real life situations, many of which do not lend themselves to simplification by ruthless abstraction. And, although the capacity of main stores has increased greatly it still falls far short of what could be used in practice.

Somewhat related to the speed factor is reliability, for some admittedly extreme applications turn on how much processing can be completed between faults. The advent of LSI has vastly improved the reliability of electronics, and its cheapness also makes it economic to duplicate key circuits. This technique of *redundancy* in circuit and system design can be extended to the use of three parallel circuits whose outputs are continuously compared; when one fails, the fact that the other two agree identifies the faulty one, and a democratic decision is taken to switch it out of circuit, and to inform the maintenance engineer. So far, redundancy has been little used in computer design, but the economic trend is towards more reliability and fewer engineers. Already, it is the electro-mechanical peripherals and ancillary equipments which break down rather than the much more complex CPU, and the attention of designers is being focussed on converting th to electronic form. The decreasing cost of electronics makes feasible to employ the principle of redundancy in the design of *error-detecting* and *error-correcting codes* for the representation of data in the system, and every transfer between th peripherals and the main store is checked to ensure that unsuspected errors do not remain to invalidate the results.

One current limitation is set by our primitive methods of placing and finding data in the main store. The most natural way would be to search our files in terms of the contents of store locations rather than the addresses which we arbitrarily attach to them. Work is, indeed, in progress on *associative stores* of this kind, but so far they have been of very limited capacity. Associative stores require more, and more complex, electronics, but the falling cost and rising reliability of integrated circuits is making this requirement acceptable.

It is a commonplace that computers have no notion of how to compute, and that when left to themselves they either sulk or generate rubbish. We have to program them, and at present we have to do this by preparing highly specific and stupefyingly detailed lists of instructions that cover every foreseeable contingency. This most demanding requirement adds greatly to the cost of computing, and greatly restricts the number of people able to use computers without going through that troublesome intermediary the programmer: it thus imposes a substantial restriction on their wider use. We have made little headway with the design of effective and convenient problem-oriented languages, which should be transparent to the user in the commoner areas of application in business and industry, but we can look forward to progress here, given time and effort.

There are three related applications where the effectiveness of today's computers is distinctly limited, namely: pattern recognition, machine translation and information retrieval. They are backward in part because today's computers are rather primitive devices - boys being used on men's work - and in part because we ourselves know little or nothing about the ways in which we recognize patterns, translate languages and retrieve information. How severe a limitation this is becomes plain when we reflect that the definition and detection of patterns underlies that recognition of speech and hand writing which would vastly increase the convenience of using computers and even more importantly, that it is a fundamental element of so much of our work, in science and economics in particular. Progress here could be of profound methodological significance as well as immediate practical value: but this very fact indicates that it is unlikely to be swift.

A final limitation on the expanding use of computers derives from our innate conservatism; we tend to resist change, even from worse to better; and any new system has to surmount a wall of opposition built from fear of the unfamiliar, and devised as a defence of well-entrenched positions. Ruts are cosy to rest in, and few of us welcome exposure to the chilly winds of change.

7.2.2 *Limitations of principle.* The limitations that we have been considering derive from current and perhaps transient deficiencies in technique, which we can hope to remedy: there are others that appear to be of a more fundamental and lasting kind. Thus, electrical signals cannot travel faster than the speed of propagation of electromagnetic waves in free space (equal to the speed of light, 3×10^8 metres/sec.), nor outside the pages of science fiction do we know of any faster method of signalling. The electronic gates whose opening and closing determine the action of a computer, currently operate in times of the order of 1 nanosec. (10^{-9} sec.), and in this time an electrical signal travels rather less than 1 ft. (300 mm) over the connecting wires between gates. To go faster, computer electronics has to be made smaller so that the distances are reduced, but clearly we face an eventual limit to miniaturization, and this will set a limit to our computing speed unless we can arrange to work on several parts of our problem in parallel. It may happen that we shall be able to exploit parallelism because we deal for the most part with weakly-coupled systems, or at any rate because we fragment the world into separate sub-systems for easier analysis. But we have little understanding of how much parallelism is possible, or whether it is confined to certain classes of problems, and if so whether these are those of most importance to us.

Again, our use of computers is currently limited to situations which can be expressed and analysed in metrical terms, for digital data has a heavy numerical content. If this were to continue it would limit the use of computers where subjective, qualitative judgements are involved as in medicine, in personnel and social work, and in the arts. These are large territories, and ones of some importance to men and women. It is tempting to note that the action of computers resembles that of our brains in the metrical areas, and so to argue that when we understand our mental processes more clearly we will be able to mimic their non-metrical activity also. But, that seems to assume that a human brain is capable of understanding itself: perhaps it can, but it is not obvious why such an ability should have been evolved, for it would have had little survival value for our ancestors.

More than a century ago Lady Lovelace wrote that a computer "... has no pretensions whatever to originate anything. It can do whatever we know how to order it to perform". This expresses a singularly tiresome limitation, for it appears to deny us the help of computers where we most need it. Certainly, it explains our lack of progress with pattern recognition; we simply do not know how we do it ourselves, hence we are not able to write down the necessary orders. It accounts also for our distinctly modest achievements in weather and economic forecasting; we are far from clear about the factors and relationships involved in these two subjects. However, we need not abandon hope, for Lady Lovelace's dictum does not rule out our writing a program that would cause a computer to assess the results of executing it, and use its assessment in modifying the program to make it more and more effective. In short, it might be possible to program a computer 'to learn from its own experience', and in this way to surpass what we could have written for it to obey; we could then raise our sights from the pettifogging detail of methods and train them on results, concentrating on ends instead of bogging down in the means.

Perhaps the limitation is not on learning but on creativity and originality, as Lady Lovelace suggested. From one point of view it is a good thing that when we have programmed a computer it does precisely what we (should have) expected, and nothing more. The same applies to men and women - too creative accountants go to gaol! Once again, part of our problem is that we are shamefully ignorant about how we ourselves invent and create. In one respect a computer is well placed to invent, for its superior speed allows it to deduce and produce every possible implication of a given set of premisses: but exhaustive analysis is not enough, the computer will not itself choose the premisses, and even though it may produce results that surprise and please us it cannot itself select those which will, and invention essentially consists in identifying which implications - if any - are significant. The element of surprise can be enhanced by using a random generator to introduce data that produce a changing and unpredictable set of results. We could in this way generate displays of coloured dots on the screen of a colour television tube connected to a computer, and we might enjoy some of these as a kind of abstract art, but it seems unlikely that we could program the machine with a set of aesthetic criteria to select only the 'artistic' and to reject the much greater volume of trivia.

130

The lack of creativity in our computers is an aspect of their passivity; they wait, fortunately, to receive our instructions, and having executed them they stop. They are not able to cope with the unforeseen, nor do they help us directly to choose what work they should do, or how they do it, nor what aims to seek. Whether they could become more self-motivated we may conveniently consider under the heading of machine 'intelligence'.

7.3 *Machine intelligence* [1,2,3]

7.3.1 *The appearance of intelligence.* The initial response of the popular press to computers was to dub them 'electronic brains', and to speculate wildly about the awesome consequences of their taking over all of our decisions and most of our thinking. Cartoonists attempt to epitomize the reactions of the average man and woman; and they invariably portrayed computers as sinister mechanical giants dominating tiny human figures. We have advanced since then, and it is now only the more frivolous journalists who write up 'computer mistakes' - usually data or system errors, in order to reassure their readers about the innate superiority of human common sense. Lady Lovelace commented: "In considering any new subject, there is frequently a tendency, first, to overrate what we find to be already interesting or remarkable; and, secondly, by a sort of natural reaction to undervalue the true state of the case when we do discover that our notions have surpassed those that are really tenable". The straightforward use of computers is now accepted as a matter of everyday routine, but we may be about to see the same attitudes recur in the development and use of machine intelligence.

However, before we embark on this subject we must attempt to reach a clear idea of what is meant by 'intelligence' in this context, so that we will know it if we should meet it. It is even more than usually important to do so because this topic is bedevilled by debates between opponents defending rigid points of view, rather than being a matter of constructive discussion between professional colleagues. Caricatures of the principal positions adopted will serve to point out the contrast between them. Thus, one group finds it offensive to human dignity that anyone can suggest that a mere machine could possibly display that most characteristic of human qualities - intelligent behaviour. This being so, they tend to define intelligence as ' whatever a machine cannot do'; and they are accordingly forced into a continuous rearguard action in which position after position has to be abandoned to the machines. The opposite group, which naturally includes those who are working in the field, is convinced that little by little computer systems will mimic most or all of the behaviour that we are accustomed to call 'intelligent'; and they regard their opponents as muddled diehards.

In this controversy there are resemblances to past debates in biology between the mechanists and the vitalists, and to current debates in psychology between Skinner behaviourists and others. Each side suspects its opponents' motives - to preserve a 'false' uniqueness for man, or to protect a pet research project - and their exchanges have the flavour of religious disputation rather than scientific discussion. Between the extreme parties we find agnostics, sceptical of many of the claims made in the name of machine intelligence, but not convinced that its pursuit is a delusion.

To begin with a simple piece of ground clearance, an 'intelligent terminal' does not qualify under this head, for the term is no more than an ill-fitting colloquialism that flatters rather than describes the behaviour of those instruments. A system exhibiting intelligent behaviour might well include

132

intelligent terminals, but its intelligence would not derive
from them; their use indicates no more than that, for economic
or operational reasons, some of the total processing power of
the system has been dispersed from the central computer to the
periphery.

What then, should we expect to be the distinguishing features of machine intelligence? In human terms, intelligence
indicates a general ability to respond to a wide range of
changing circumstances in a flexible and appropriate manner.
By analogy we would expect the responses of an intelligent
machine system to show signs of conscious adaptation based on a
rational evaluation of the needs of the situation: 'conscious'
does not necessarily imply 'self-conscious', but only that the
response is more than a predetermined reflex action. It follows that it would not be sufficient for a computer system to
hold a dictionary of standard responses to all foreseen situations, and simply to look up the nearest fit and apply it:
this might be called 'instinctive', but not intelligent, behaviour. There needs to be an element of learning from experience. Learning, of course, is more than just remembering,
a tape recorder can do that, it means also modifying the tactics and strategy expressed in the programs that control the
system's responses, and doing so in the light of the results
achieved. And, the assessment of success, plus the consequent
changes in programs, would have to be carried out automatically
by the system itself.

The ability to learn is a necessary, but not a sufficient,
indicator of intelligence; merely to respond to events is too
passive, and we would expect to see the machine correlates of
curiosity and purposefulness. Given these, the system would
probe its assigned environment, and attempt to predict and
anticipate the course of relevant events in it: and, when conditions were static, but its goal remained unachieved, it would

make exploratory forays, either by altering its control variables at random, or by sweeping them systematically over a suitable range, and it would then assess the consequences in terms of progress towards the nominated goal. The next stage of development might be for the system to select its own proximate goals, or sub-goals, in terms of a broad directive set by its user, but this could hardly be a required characteristic for many of us work towards goals that we have not chosen ourselves, yet we would claim that our behaviour - even at work - was intelligent.

It is worth noting at this point what machine intelligence is not. It is not the making of a complete and convincing simulacrum of a human being, the android of science fiction. Featherless bipedalism is not the only route to intelligent behaviour. Nor is it the construction of a robot that is a *general* replacement for a man, without necessarily looking like one. It is not even the complete simulation of a human correspondent at the other end of a telecommunication link. Turing, indeed, proposed to answer the related question 'Can machines think?' by an 'imitation game' in which a human interrogator, A, telephoned questions to a man and a woman, X and Y, located in a separate room. The object of the game is for A to discover which of X and Y is the woman. Turing considered that if Y were replaced by a computer (suitably programmed, of course) and that computer succeeded in convincing A that it was the woman, then it could be said to 'think'. But, an ability to score points in conversational gamesmanship is not the *only* way in which a machine system could display intelligent behaviour, that is, could be said to have 'thought' before acting.

In short, a machine system would not need to match every capability of human beings before it could validly be judged to exhibit machine intelligence. It would be sufficient for it to show in some particular field of application those characteristics of intelligent behaviour that we have already discussed.

7.3.2 *Why work on machine intelligence?* Some critics see those who work on machine intelligence as latter-day Frankensteins whose monsters, even if they were to be created, would serve no useful purpose. From this somewhat prejudicial premiss they argue that the work is at best a frivolous diversion from the real business of computer science, which is to develop new techniques and apply them to the pressing problems of users, and at worst, a serious misapplication of talent. Like much of the discussion of this topic, this is too partial to be true. A number of reasons can be advanced in favour of pushing the development of machine intelligence as far as it will go.

(a) The classic justification for all research, namely that the problem has been posed, and cannot be argued out of existence.

(b) Machine intelligence would have direct use in self-adapting and self-optimizing systems for the control of industrial processes, air and road traffic, telecommunications, and so on; and it might be the only way of making progress in these applications.

(c) Machine intelligence could probably make significant contributions to the solution of such troublesome and important problems as pattern recognition, information retrieval, and predicting the behaviour of complex systems.

(d) The work could conceivably throw a revealing sidelight on the way in which our own brains work, thus benefiting science and medicine, as well as being of considerable philosophical interest.

(e) There is a rather speculative possibility that by constructing powerful and complex systems we might be able to produce a level of machine intelligence that exceeds our own, in specific and limited areas, and which we could bring to bear on problems now beyond our competence.

(f)   The common, but somewhat desperate, claim of those seeking research funds that the spin-off (anyway) will be of incalculable value; certainly, it is usually rather easy to agree that no one can calculate it. However, it is true that computing techniques are likely to be most improved by tackling problems that lie at the edge of the possible.

7.3.3 *Some areas of work on machine intelligence.* The playing of games is a simplistic imitation of our competitive struggles with each other and with our environment, and noughts and crosses, Nim, draughts and chess have received attention as games fit for computers to play. Shannon distinguished four types of game-playing machines – apart from those that conceal a dwarf.

(a)   Those holding a dictionary of all possible moves and responses.

(b)   Those for games with a calculable formula for successful play.

(c)   Those that apply general principles of approximate validity.

(d)   Learning machines, programmed with the rules and strategies of the game, and capable of analysing their play and that of their opponents in order to improve their achievement.

Of these, (a) is practicable only for very simple determinate games – such as noughts and crosses; (b) can be used for Nim; (c) can play a modest game of draughts or chess; but only (d) qualifies as machine intelligence. International chess matches are now being held between computer programs, and in 1974 the Russian program 'Kaissa' won the tournament. So far, such programs are ineffective against chess masters, but they can often

136

beat lesser players by being quick, accurate, consistent and free from emotional hang-ups. It is quite impossible to play chess by an exhaustive evaluation of every possible move and counter-move; chess-playing programs use *heuristic* methods, that is, evaluated trial and error, to reduce the number of alternatives to be examined.

The application of learning techniques to pattern recognition is being pursued in a number of areas, for example: the reading of printed and hand written texts, the recognition of spoken words, the identification of finger prints, the detection of pathogenic agents, and the examination of air photographs. As well as its potential practical value, this work has considerable theoretical significance for it bears on the formation and definition of general concepts; to take a simple example, the A-ness of all A's. This is a fundamental human activity that permeates all our rational thought, and the ability to form concepts would be a strong indicator of 'intelligence'.

The problems associated with creativity arise in work on computer art. Thus, computers have been used to write poetry, to compose music and to 'paint' abstract pictures; but all of this has been by a rather mechanical application of rules for the combination of standard elements. It, therefore, fails to touch the key problem, which is how to detect the small amount of gold among the mass of dross: it is all too easy to generate enormous volumes of material, but we do not yet understand how we select from it what, if any, is significant. If this problem were to be solved by a machine system, then it, too, would have a strong claim to intelligence, for as Chesterton once wrote: "Art is the signature of man".

For a great many years robots have fascinated inventors, and a number of laboratories are working on these devices. The work is in its earliest stages and the experimental situ-

ations inevitably suggest a rather childish playing with mechanical toys: the choice of a representative environment and
task for test purposes is not an easy one, for its characteristics will in some measure determine the problems thrown up,
and in this way bias the direction of the research. It is
clear that the design of an integrated robot poses major problems of machine intelligence, and current work is directed at
these rather than at the production of robots as such. It is
often as difficult in research to find the right problems as
it is to find the right solutions, but those working on robots have little trouble in finding problems! First, there
are severe problems associated with processing the data from
the robot's visual perception, taking account of the changes
in viewpoint as it moves itself, and also manipulates objects
near it. There are more problems in the design of the tactics
and strategies for the exploration of the environment, the
pursuit of the set goals, and the adaptation of strategy by a
learning process.

7.3.4 *Machine intelligence and man.* If it should prove to be
possible to develop machine intelligence for everyday use we
need not expect this to pose any serious threat to men and
women. It seems unlikely that it will be economic to make
completely general-purpose systems of this kind, and machine
intelligence is likely to take a range of specialized forms.
In their specialist areas such machines will be able to offer
us invaluable help, with no risk of their trespassing outside
of their assigned activity and usurping other, wider, function
We may sum up the relationship in a rather horrid piece of terminology by saying that the complementary roles of human and
machine intelligence would allow them to combine in a syner-
gistic symbiosis, in which we will find the problems and the
machines will find the answers.

7.4 *Bibliography*

A number of articles on machine intelligence and robotics, by Turing, von Neumann, Shannon and others, are conveniently collected in:

(1) *Perspectives on the Computer Revolution*, ed. Z.W. Pylyshyn. Prentice Hall, 1970.

And, the differences between computers and our brains are discussed in:

(2) *The Computer and the Brain*, by J. von Neumann. Yale Univ. Press, 1958.

In reading this book and the next the techniques need to be updated, but the main argument is not affected. The arguments against the more extravagant machine intelligence - giant brains advocates appear in:

(3) *Computers and Common Sense: The Myth of Thinking Machines*, by Mortimer Taube. Columbia Univ. Press, 1961.

Examples 7

(7.1) Qualitative judgments are unavoidable in many applications; suggest how they might be recorded and processed by a digital computer, illustrating your answer with reference to an example drawn from, say, medicine or personnel work. What difficulties would you expect to arise in practice?

(7.2) "Money spent on machine translation, say between Russian and English, would be better spent on training men and women as interpreters". Give your reasons for agreeing or disagreeing with this statement.

(7.3) At least for many years, it is unlikely that any computer system displaying machine intelligence would be able to score highly in a conventional IQ test. Assuming this to be so, what conclusions does it suggest about these tests, and about machine intelligence?

(7.4) Discover from the literature how many cells (neurons) are believed to exist in the human brain, and how many logical elements (gates) there are in a typical digital computer. Discuss any implications that these figures suggest. The data about the number of cells in the brai has been copied from text to text, determine - if you can - the date of the original observations on which the estimate is based.

(7.5) Indicate what benefits we may hope to obtain from research into machine intelligence.

(7.6) In what respects would you expect a machine system show ing machine intelligence to fall short of human behaviou

(7.7) How may the very high speed of calculation of digital computers assist our understanding of economics?

(7.8) "Pattern recognition is the basis of all our activities Is this statement true? false? Or trivial?

(7.9) Develop a simple arithmetical argument to suggest why a computer cannot play successful chess by the exhaustive evaluation of every possible move and countermove.

(7.10) A computer can control a machine tool to produce complex metal components. Why can it not produce an origin piece of sculpture in metal?

8 · Computers and the professions

8.1 *Computers and the professional*

Before we attempt to consider the effects of computers on professional work we need to settle what we mean by a profession. Traditionally, the term was applied to the Church, the Law and Medicine; and it has been extended to a wide variety of modern disciplines. It implies a degree of dedication to an intellectual task, combined with a sense of responsibility to the client and to society that goes beyond the requirements of the average commercial relationship.

The client benefits, because he is served by someone jealous of his technical integrity, and pledged not to do a shoddy job. Society benefits, because the professional's clients are steered away from faulty and inadequate practices and towards accepted norms; and also because the profession accepts responsibility for developing and guarding an important part of society's common culture. The professional himself benefits, because society affords him a respected status in the community. Given these all-round advantages, it is not surprising that professions flourish, and proliferate as new fields are opened up. Nor is it surprising that the well-established professions adhere tenaciously to the ground they already occupy; they are keenly aware that new professions tend to sprout in the cracks between them. Computing itself aspires to professional status, as its institutions show, but it is not yet clear whether it is an independent subject in its own right or just an auxiliary skill, such as the ability to write and calculate.

The use of computers in professional work has so far bee
supplementary: thus, engineers use them to calculate more con
prehensively than was previously practicable, and doctors use
them to store and recall medical records. However, there is
now a considerable number of program packages which allow les
experienced, or less-competent, professionals to use advanced
techniques and up-to-date information which were previously
the preserve of the upper flights of the profession. Extra-
polation of this trend suggests that such methods will also b
come available for amateurs to use - providing them with clip
on skills and instant competence. There are evident dangers
extending this process, for professional skill consists not
only in applying powerful techniques, but also in being able
judge their relevance, and in knowing their limitations. Ne
theless, the continued growth of computer aids is bound to af
ect the work of professionals: within a profession they will
tend to equalize the level of skill, by raising the lowest; a
they may remove some of the more straightforward problems fro
the professional area altogether.

The supplementary nature of computing in professional wo
needs to be continually borne in mind, and for this purpose t
invariable use of the word 'aided' after the word 'computer'
most valuable, as in computer-aided design, or computer-aide
diagnosis. This is no trivial stylistic point, for it is al
too easy to fall into the trap of thinking like the headline
writers who proclaim that computers *are* designing bridges, de
ciding medical treatment and so on. What is happening is ra
the same separation of skills that arises when automatic mac
ery is used in manufacturing. Thus, in a furniture factory t
craft skill of the cabinet maker is replaced by the higher s
of the professional production engineer and the lower skill o
the plant operators. Routine engineering design, for example
is barely a professional activity, and it is being replaced b

142

the higher skill of the theoretician who writes the package program, and the lower skills of the computer operators. Members of all professions can expect to be relieved of the routine chores of their disciplines, and thus be freed to make more creative and individual contributions; but whether all of them will welcome working continuously at the top of their form remains to be seen: undemanding routine calculation is a habit-forming way of relaxing while appearing to be hard at work.

Lady Lovelace made many pertinent comments on the future art of computing, and she shrewdly observed that in the course of the analyses needed to make our problems "easily and rapidly amenable to the mechanical combinations of the engine, the relations and nature of many subjects .... are necessarily thrown into new lights, and more profoundly investigated". In writing a program a professional is forced to take the computer's detailed worm's-eye view of his subject, in contrast to the by and large bird's-eye view more congenial to men and women, and this could have valuable by-products. To put the same thought in different terms, there is a well worn saying that the best way to learn a subject is to teach it to someone else; well, no pupil could be more exacting than a computer, and by the time you have successfully programmed a problem you can be sure that you really have understood it. The most valuable characteristic of computers is not that they are electronic brains, which they are not, but that they make *us* think, and think harder than we have ever thought before.

8.2 *Some professional uses reviewed*

8.2.1 *Science.* Scientists use computers in the development of theory, the conduct of experiments and the analysis of results. The theoretician's applications are mostly arithmetical, and relate to trial calculations designed to test a tentative hypothesis. Some progress is, however, being made with the use of computers for reducing complex algebraic expressions, and in this their freedom from error throughout a long deductive chain is particularly valuable. Crystallography is an area which has been revolutionized by the use of computers for the analysis of X-ray diffraction patterns involves arith metic on a most massive scale. Before 1950 it was a major fe to deal with crystals of up to 20 atoms, but today crystals with more than 1000 atoms present few problems. Program packages are available for crystallographic work which can perform in 12 minutes calculations that would take 12 months by hand.

The public image of science is one of smooth precision and relentlessly successful advance: the reality of experimen tal work is that when the apparatus is as complex as it usually is the scientist spends most of his time in keeping it 'on the verge of operation' - to adopt Lord Bowden's vivid phrase. Much time can be wasted in abortive observations whe the apparatus is misbehaving, and that is not always obvious until the results have been analysed. When a computer can be connected on-line to the apparatus to analyse the results as they come in, it can most valuably indicate when things begin to go wrong.

The processing of results on-line also speeds the rhythm of research by avoiding the need to interrupt experimental work while the day's results are digested. The final step is to use the computer to control the experiment directly. Thus to draw a simple example from applied science, the developmen of reliable semi-conductor devices involves taking thousands of measurements on hundreds of specimens over long periods. The connection of the specimen to the measuring heads can be automatically controlled by a computer in terms of the observed change in parameters since the previous measurement, so that measurements are made at shorter intervals when the observed rate of change is large.

8.2.2 *Engineering*. Engineering design often involves very large calculations; for example, when designing a bridge it is important to calculate the stresses and strains in every member. Before computers were available this was just not practicable for the time and cost were both prohibitive, and rather gross simplifications were common – and large factors of safety (or ignorance) were necessary. Now, it is not only possible to make the detailed calculations but even to repeat them for a range of alternative conditions, for example to explore the effect of high winds from various directions, or for alternative designs, in order to discover the most economic structure. Designers are being relieved of routine work, for when standard formulae, methods and materials are good enough the computer can be programmed to make the appropriate calculations, and even to optimize the design.

The foregoing example of computer aided design (CAD) is drawn from civil engineering, but computers are invaluable in engineering of every kind. Mechanical engineers use them to design springs, gears and other machine parts; electrical engineers to design motors and transformers; electronic engineers to design integrated circuits, and chemical engineers to design the complicated pipe work of a process plant. Production engineers use automatic machine tools to shape complex metal parts, and these tools are guided in terms of the numerical coordinates of key points and the lines which connect them, and this information is recorded on control tapes. Specialist POL's are available for writing programs which interpret a geometrical design and generate the corresponding control tape for a specified numerically-controlled machine tool.

A great deal of engineering design is concerned as much with diagrams as it is with numerical data, and the light pen and cathode-ray-tube display are powerful instruments of CAD. The key points of a structure can be delineated, and their coordinates stored. The associated computer can then re-compute the shape of the structure as it would appear from a different viewing point, and by doing so repeatedly for a series of viewpoints around the circumference of a circle the depiction of the structure seems to rotate, thus allowing it to be examined in the round. This facility is of particular value in the design of objects whose appearance is important, for instance, car bodies. Here, having achieved a pleasing shape, the computer can calculate strengths and weights so that the designer may adjust his design to meet safety and production requirements while observing the effects on appearance.

Engineering design is rarely a once-for-all process; designs are commonly amended over the years to take account of difficulties in manufacture, or in service, or because some bought-in component ceases to be available. Amendment can involve altering dozens of related drawings in which an item features; and making sure that every affected drawing is identified and altered, and that no problems arise, is a major task that absorbs a lot of time in design offices. By keeping the master 'drawings' in digital form in a computer file amendments can be tried out and assessed.

8.2.3 *Medicine.* Computers can obviously be used to keep medical records, and for the ordinary office work of hospitals and surgeries. Clearly, there would be merit in keeping a person's complete medical history in a single file which could be interrogated from anywhere over a telecommunications link. Some medical work would also be helped if the medical records of a complete family could be readily linked together. Both of these proposals, however, raise problems of economics and of privacy; and neither is likely to progress very rapidly.

Attempts have been made to bring computers to the aid of diagnosis, by using them to sift and collate the results of laboratory tests and clinical observations. Medicine is not yet sufficiently codified for diagnosis to be a completely determinate procedure; there is no unique correspondence between sets of signs and symptoms and diseases, and perhaps as biological materials we are too variable. The computer can, therefore, do no more than indicate a range of possibilities, and the tests that would help to decide between them. Its role is like that of a pilot: when entering harbour a ship's master does well to heed the pilot's advice, for he could be in serious trouble if he did not, but the responsibility remains firmly with the master.

In Leicester, a computer system supports the management of the home nursing service by keeping records with details of treatments, and by scheduling the nurses' visits, taking account of the times needed for treatments and for travelling. Computers are used also in intensive care units, in which the patient is fitted out with measuring devices to indicate his respiration rate, temperature, blood pressure, heart function and so on. These devices are connected on-line to a computer programmed to analyse their readings and detect any dangerous pattern of variation in them; and the patient is thus watched over by an alert, unsleeping, vigilant electronic nurse. Computers can be used on-line to monitor an anaesthetized patient undergoing a major operation. In some forms of radio-therapy the calculation of dosage is difficult, as when the radio-active source is rotated continuously around a patient in order to maximize the exposure of the diseased part, and minimize that of the surrounding healthy tissue. The calculations are tedious, but a computer can make short work of them, save the time of medical technicians, and reduce the risk of error.

147

8.2.4 *Education*. Computer aided instruction (CAI) exploits the use of remote terminals, often VDU's, operating in conversational mode. The operation stands or falls on the merits of programmed learning, for the computer is simply the means for increasing its convenience to the pupil. There is also a psychological factor, in that children - and some others - like the feeling of being in control of powerful technical equipment of advanced design; moreover, an unemotional, unprovokable, unimaginably patient, machine may be able to capture their interest, stimulate their imagination and hold their attention more successfully than can a jaded and overworked teacher.

CAI is one facet of educational technology, a market vacuum which electronic salesmen seem anxious to fill, and there is a danger in any new subject that it will be dominated by cranks, and fall prey to instant experts. In education particularly, it is vital that we stress the word 'aided', and insist that what is done is directed by those long experienced in education, and not by those newly expert in computing.

A specialized form of education is industrial training, for instance, the training of an airline's pilots in readiness for a new type of aircraft. Pre-flight training can take place in a simulator in which the pilot sits in a mock-up of the new cockpit, complete with all instruments and controls. The cockpit can be moved or vibrated by hydraulic jacks, and there are appropriate aural and visual effects. All of these are linked on-line to a computer which responds to the pilot's actions, and which is programmed to simulate the conditions and emergencies that he would experience in flying the new aircraft over a particular route, or into a chosen airport. Simulation training is possible even before the aircraft is built, and can be used experimentally in order to eliminate design faults, or evaluate alternatives. Simulation programs have also been used

to train medical students, and computer operators, and there
is no reason other than economics why they should not be used
universally.

8.2.5 *The law.* Computers are widely used in law enforcement,
and have been applied more tentatively to the work of the courts
and of legislation. These last raise the broader and still un-
resolved problems of information retrieval, for with the whole
corpus of the law recorded a computer could perform valuable
services in searching for statutes and precedents. In legislation also, some have suggested that a computer could be used
to test new proposals by assessing the consequences of applying
them to past cases. It would be feasible to check statutes for
anomalies and inconsistencies, and to indicate where rational-
ization is required.

   Law enforcement rests on an efficient police force, and
computers are widely used for many police purposes, including:
(a)   the management and control of police operations;
(b)   providing information to policemen on foot patrol and in
      cars;
(c)   criminal records;
(d)   wanted and missing persons files;
(e)   lists of stolen property and vehicles;
(f)   vehicle and driver's licence records;
(g)   investigation of patterns of criminal behaviour.
As in all police work, there is an inherent tension between an
individual's right to liberty and privacy and society's duty to
ensure that the majority of its members can live in freedom from
the consequences of criminal behaviour by the anti-social few.
The keeping in computer files of personal data of all kinds -
demographic, economic, medical and financial, as well as criminal, raises questions about individual privacy which are taken
up in chapter 10.

8.2.6 *National defence*. Like other large organizations the armed forces use computers for the management of men and resources. They use them also to process data from radars, sonars and other sources of military information in order to present a complete and up-to-date picture of the battle situation. Computers are used on-line to control automatic weapon systems. They are also used in training, where they make it possible to play war games of great complexity, and on a scale and with a realism impossible in the days of sand-trays and TEWTs - tactical exercises without troops. None of these uses is uniquely military, for all of them are duplicated in civil environments characterized by intense competition and imperfect information, for example, in business and industry.

8.2.7 *Literature*. Nothing demonstrates the fact that computers are not limited to calculation more clearly than their use in text processing. At the purely mechanical level, a scientific paper, a business report, or even a poem can be written directly through the keyboard of a VDU directly onto a magnetic disk, recalled for display and altered or corrected by processing the stored data. Material can be inserted or deleted, the order of paragraphs can be rearranged and standard items can be incorporated without the need for extensive retyping. When the text is complete it can be processed by a program whose output is a magnetic tape that controls a typesetting machine directly, thus setting the text up in print without the need for further human intervention, or the risk of copying errors.

At a more literary level, computers have been used to process magnetic recordings of texts in order to produce an index or a concordance, thus saving days, or even years, of scholarly drudgery. Some years ago, scandalized headlines proclaimed that a computer had dared to challenge St. Paul's

authorship of certain New Testament epistles. The reality
was more prosaic, but the example serves to underline what
should be an obvious point. The computer had been used in
statistical studies of the vocabulary used in the Greek text,
as a guide to literary style, and whether or not the results
argued for or against St. Paul depended not at all on the
fact that a computer happened to have been used, but on:

(a) the validity of the literary hypothesis that an author
can be identified by counting the frequency with which
he uses some of the commoner words;

(b) the acceptability of the historical evidence that St.
Paul wrote any of the texts examined.

Similar studies have been made for other classical works of
disputed authorship, notably the Federalist Papers, and the
method has evident application to history as well as to literature.

8.2.8 *Economics.* Computers are now indispensable to economists
for statistical work, but their most significant application is
in the analysis of model systems. Modelling is a topic of general interest, and is taken up in a wider context in the next
section.

8.3 *Computer-driven models*

8.3.1 *The development of models.* The construction of theoretical models to explain and predict natural phenomena is well
established as a scientific technique[2], and is used in the study
of economic and environmental systems. A model consists of a
set of mathematical and logical relationships which express the
interactions between the principal factors believed to affect
the situation being studied. As our investigations get to grip
with the untidy complexity of real life we have to bring more

and more factors into account, and we find that their relatio
are more or less non-linear, have thresholds and ceilings, ar
non-numeric, or probabilistic, or elude the grasp of formal
analysis in a variety of mathematically unpleasant ways. But
provided we can specify an unambiguous relationship we can wr
a program to express it.

We can also use a computer to help us to simplify our
models by eliminating the less relevant factors. This is ach
ieved by *sensitivity analyses* in which a factor is varied ove
its full range, for this will show how sensitive the result i
to change in it. Ideally, we should conduct sensitivity test
on all possible pairs and combinations of factors to look for
non-linear couplings between them, but this counsel of perfec
tion is rarely followed. Similar test runs can explore a ran
of coefficients in equations, or alternative forms of relatio
between factors. Indeed, trial runs of the model provide a
valuable surrogate for experiment in subjects such as economi
where laboratory work or field trials are impracticable. And
when we consider the effect on the development of the physica
sciences when experiment replaced speculation it seems possib
that even substitute experiment may profoundly influence the
development of the non-experimental disciplines.

It is not enough to be able to identify which are the re
levant factors, it is necessary also to be able to measure th
with sufficient accuracy. Sensitivity analysis can help here
as well, for if, say, a 1% change in the factor is found to
produce no more than an insignificant change in the result,
then there is little point in straining to measure it to ± 0.

8.3.2 *Some problems*. The accuracy of the available data is a
important practical limitation on the use of models. Economi
data, in particular, are often very much less accurate than i
implied by the precision to which they are quoted[1]. For in-

stance, the annual rate of growth of the Gross National Product is widely canvassed as a key economic indicator, and is often quoted with ± 0.1% precision; but it can scarcely be measured to an accuracy of ± 1%. Morgenstern has provided many such examples of illusory precision. Again, data collected for one purpose may be unthinkingly applied to another, without examining the assumptions built into the original method of measurement: we tend to assume that facts are facts, without realizing that every fact rests on a base of theory, often fossilized theory that we have ceased to challenge. In economics again, important data may not be available at all, and we then have to fall back on estimates - or worse, on someone's judgement, when the data are not amenable to quantification.

Another limitation derives from the theoretical relationships expressed in the model. In some areas we simply do not know enough to be able to propose a plausible set of relationships for study. Moreover, some models are sensitive creatures; and their results can depend super-critically on the data and parameter values used: when, therefore, we are too confident about our chosen values their results can mislead, and when we attempt to explore over a realistic range the result oscillates wildly.

In theoretical work we usually reach a satisfactory understanding of static equilibrium states before we can handle the dynamics of transitions between equilibria. Life, however, is never steady-state, and some transient situations are accompanied by disturbingly large fluctuations. Difficulty with the dynamics is particularly to be expected when the model merely describes the phenomena without attempting to explain them, as when it is content to remain with the mathematics rather than seek out causes. *Systems Dynamics* offers a causal approach to modelling which strives to cover all the processes of adaptation and self-regulation in a system, and focusses on dynamic behaviour by analysing its feedback loops.

8.3.3 *Some dangers.* The most obvious danger is that important
matters, such as economics, may fall into the hands of 'academ
theory-mongers. As we have suggested above, economic data are
incomplete, none too reliable, and subject to fallible interpretation; and economic theory itself expresses a point of vie
rather than an established body of doctrine. Nevertheless, th
use of a powerful analytic technique, and the spurious precisi
deriving from the use of an expensive computer may lull us int
the false belief that the results are beyond challenge by our
unaided common sense. We need to repeat three times daily tha
no computer model can be better than the mental model on which
it is based, or the data with which it is supplied. Fortunately, the average man, and even more the average woman, regards
all experts as more or less mad.

Most of our theories and models deal with the totality of
the real life situation by carving it up into 'independent' su
systems. This is a methodological necessity rather than a fac
of nature, for although computers vastly enlarge our power of
handling many variables, they do not enlarge our ability to co
ceive the pattern of relationships between them. Before computer modelling we knew our limitations and we simplified ruth
lessly; we have not hitherto had to think in complex total-
system terms, and in doing so we have no alternative but to
learn from experience, and we can expect to make some ripe old
hashes in the process.

8.3.4 *Some uses of models.* The examples cited have been econo
mic, and indeed many micro-economic models of individual firms
and macro-economic models of a nation, or even of the whole
world, have been constructed and used to guide, or alarm, thos
who make decisions. Modelling has long been used in science

154

and engineering, for instance, to predict the behaviour of the tides, of an electrical energy distribution network, or of a telecommunication switching system. It is being used to plan city transport, to study physiological processes and to assess social interactions; and it is the basis of war and business games.

Modelling is, without doubt, an intellectual tool of very great power and wide-ranging application. Let us, therefore, remember: first John Culkin's comment that "We shape our tools, and then they shape us"; and second, Whitehead's advice to "Seek simplicity, and distrust it". Our models are only models, and we must not mistake them for the real world; we must use them with wary optimism. They do, after all, leave out the most important variable of all - ourselves[3,4,5].

8.4 *Bibliography*

The general theme of the professions and the computer is dealt with in the scattered publications of the separate professional societies; and the computer press provides a running stream of information about all kinds of applications to professional work. On accuracy see:

(1) *On the Accuracy of Economic Observations*, by Oskar Morgenstern. Princeton University Press, 2nd ed. 1963.
In the specific matter of modelling:
(2) *Models and Analogies in Science*, by Mary B. Hesse. Sheed and Ward, 1963. Deals with the role of models in science, and:
(3) *Simulation and Business Decisions*, by G.T. Jones. Penguin, 1972. Covers their use in management.
The famous, not to say notorious, world economic model of the Club of Rome is described in:
(4) *The Limits to Growth*, by D.H. Meadows, D.L. Meadows, J. Randers and W.W. Behrens. Universe Books, 1972.
And, it is criticized by the Science Policy Research Unit of

the University of Sussex in:

(5) *Thinking about the Future*, by H.S.D. Cole, C. Freeman, M. Jahoda, and K.L.R. Pavitt. Chatto and Windus, 1973. This book also contains some useful comments on modelling in general.

Examples 8

(8.1) Bernard Shaw wrote: "All professions are conspiracies against the laity". Discuss this observation, and comment on the effect of the widespread use of computers on the role and status of professional men and women.

(8.2) Computing will have different effects on, say accountan and medicine. Classify the professions according to the likely effects of computing on them, giving the reasons for your scheme.

(8.3) "Complication in the model implies realism in the results". Discuss this statement.

(8.4) Define 'precision' and 'accuracy', drawing a clear dist inction between them. Collect examples of spurious precision. Suggest reasons why pocket calculators operate with precisions in the range 8 to 12 digits.

(8.5) Say why you believe that computing is – or is not – a professional activity in its own right.

(8.6) Program packages can allow ordinary men and women to apply advanced professional methods; what problems may beset, say, a D-I-Y engineer?

(8.7) Lady Lovelace thought that programming a task might lea to new insights, and a more profound understanding of it Give your reasons for agreeing – or disagreeing – with her view.

(8.8) What are the problems of applying computers to aid the diagnosis of diseases?

(8.9) It would be feasible to link the controls of a stationa

car to a computer-controlled simulator presenting appropriate audio-visual effects to its 'driver'. Could such
a device be used to train and test learner drivers?

8.10) How far might a computer be used in Shakespearean studies?

9 · Computers in business and industry

9.1 Business applications

9.1.1 *The processing of business data*[1,2,3,4]. The difference
between scientific and commercial computing can be caricature
thus: scientific computing is like a pure mathematician calcu
lating massively, but with very little input or output; and
commercial computing is like a business executive, passing
masses of data across his desk, but with little happening to
it on the way. In business systems the input and output of
data are of key importance, and most of the computer's progra
is concerned with identifying, validating, marshalling and re
arranging this data rather than with performing calculations
with it. Other differences include:

(a) business computing is performed to improve office effici
    ency, hence costs are more important than they usually
    are in scientific work;

(b) business programs run repeatedly with many thousands of
    items, and are used over periods of many months without
    change, hence efficiency in the program is much more ne
    essary than for the ephemeral programs of much of scien
    tific computing;

(c) the profitability, indeed the survival, of a major enter
    prise depends crucially on the business computer's out
    put, hence operating and program errors incur much heav
    penalties than the waste of a few hours of computer tim

(d) business programs are very much longer and more complex
than scientific ones, which makes them harder to write
and check, and costly to produce - a rough-and-ready rule
is that it costs about as much to write the programs that
will fully load a business computer as it does to buy it,
and to put this into scale £500,000 worth of computer requires another £500,000 to be spent on systems analysis
and programming.

9.1.2 *Isolated sub-systems.* The earliest business computers
were used for straightforward accountancy; pay calculation was
a common first use, and invoicing and billing soon followed.
Since then their use has expanded enormously, as shown by the
outline sketched in below - this list is very far from being
complete, for the number of applications is legion, and grows
daily.

(a) *Securities* Investment analysis and advice, quotations
and orders for stocks and bonds, accounting.

(b) *Insurance* Quotations, policy records and status inquiries, premium and claim accounting, medi-
cal data base.

(c) *Banking and Finance* Cashier and customer inquiries about balances
and credit status, automatic cash dispensers,
cheque clearances, inter-bank transfers and
general accounting.

(d) *Manufact-uring* Accounting, including payroll and cash management, personnel records, sales and marketing,
invoicing and billing, component and materials
orders and inventory control, production planning and control, long-term planning by micro-
economic modelling.

(e) *Distribu-tion and Retailing* Wholesale warehouse inventory control, distribution schedules; point-of-sale data records
and processing for cash control, sales analysis

and retail inventory control; credit checking and general accounting.

(f) *Transport*   Vehicle, driver and service scheduling, seat reservation, freight control, general accounting.

(g) *Government*   Many government office applications mirror those of private business, for example, accounting, personnel records, inventory control. Additionally, computers are being used to keep records for taxation and licencing, national defence and police work, statistical work for the census and economic departments, and the administration of the education health, employment and social services.

(h) *Information*   These are not well developed, apart from applications to printing, and in some specialist areas – notably finance.
     Services

Sheer quantity of application is not impressive, quality of thinking in the systems is more important; and this is a product of individual ingenuity rather than the mere passage of time. Indeed, the pioneer use of a computer in a commercial office was J. Lyon & Co.'s LEO I which, as long ago as 1953 operated a clever system for supplying the firm's tea shops. Managers reported by telephone at the end of each day only what variations they required to their standard daily orders – individual to each shop, and seasonally adjusted – and this data was used to compute tomorrow's work schedules for the bakery and the delivery van fleet.

9.1.3 *Management information systems (MIS)*. It was soon realized that separate applications within one business were closely coupled: for instance, pay calculation uses data about the hours worked by employees and their attendance, which is used also in production control, and for personnel work; and

160

the resulting pay is one item of input data for the cost control system. The next stage of development was, therefore, to design integrated systems, and these require an unusually clear understanding of what office work is all about. The simple one-man business that used to grace the early chapters of economic textbooks need no offices and no formal management: but today's giant corporations have evolved, and do in fact need, a complex management machinery to regulate their activities. Managers are concerned with coordination and control; their function is to ensure that their firm reacts quickly and appropriately to the changing circumstances of its business environment, and their decisions depend heavily on the prompt supply of accurate, relevant, and up-to-date information: it is the prime task of the office staff to collect and present this information. In the course of this work they will print pay slips, make tax returns, place orders, despatch invoices, issue delivery notes and bills, prepare accounts, conduct sales surveys and analyse market prospects; but all of these activities have to be seen in the context of the process of generating the information needed for the management and control of the business.

To illustrate the computer's role we can represent the manager's task diagrammatically, as in Fig. 9.1. The MIS is shown as a part of a feedback loop in which data about the situation to be controlled are collected and, together with relevant historical data drawn from a common data base, are filtered and processed to drive a VDU display on a manager's desk. He uses the information presented to him to decide which managerial actions to take to influence the target situation. The function of the computer is to speed up and improve the presentation of information to the manager, so that his decisions can be more timely and more relevant.

The target situation is also influenced by factors that we

161

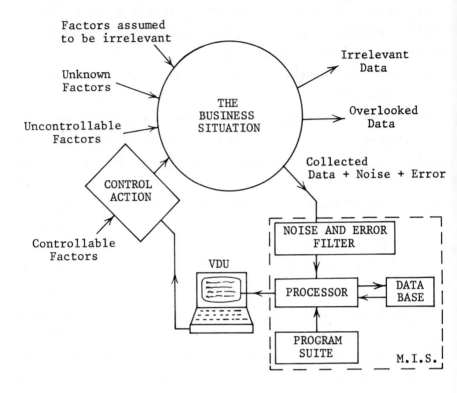

Fig. 9.1   The manager's task
(The "Noise and Error Filter" indicates the Data Vetting Stage
of Processing).

know about, but cannot control; by unknown factors, and by
others that we have judged to be irrelevant, but which may not
be entirely so. Again, as well as the data we do collect ther
will be others that we miss, or reject as unimportant. Our
programs for filtering and processing the data may be misconceived, or only partially effective, or have concealed errors:
The data will contain errors, and it is inevitably collected
in arrears. The manager has personal qualities and defects of
judgement, decisiveness and attentiveness, all of which affect
the outcome. Moreover, he will often be seeking to regulate

more than one feature of the target situation, and attempting to do so in spite of restrictions on the action he can take – either from external constraints, or from resource limitations, and these last will be different in the short and the long term. The problem of simultaneous multiple optimization within constraints is not an easy one, even when the optimization criteria are clear (as they rarely, if ever, are in business), and the controls operate smoothly, instantaneously, independently and without hysteresis (as they never do in practical affairs).

It will be evident that the design of an effective MIS is far from being a simple task, and also that situations differ in manageability. When we can know and control all the major factors, and are able to measure all the relevant data, then we have a well-regulated cybernetic system. We can also go quite a long way when we have a straightforward situation involving limited files of data, and a few, clearly defined, functions – a seat reservation system, for instance. At the far extreme we have the weather, or the national economic situation, where we neither know the theory, nor if we did could we control every significant factor. Such systems are inherently of low manageability, we might call them acybernetic, and it is as well to recognise that they exist.

Even with these reservations, computer-based management information systems have much to offer: they can analyse data and keep up with events that are too complex and too fast for human comprehension. They can indeed provide a torrent of up-to-date figures on anything and everything, and computer men tend to assume that because some information is good, more will be better. We must decide precisely what information is required for the manager's purposes, what will help him to make better business decisions; and this will depend on which of the three main levels of management he occupies thus:

(a) Strategic Planning, concerned with determining policies and objectives, and settling the broad provision and disposition of resources.

(b) Management Control, concerned with formulating work schedules, the detailed allocation of resources and the monitoring of progress.

(c) Operational Control, concerned with assigning tasks, and with supervising and reporting on the daily execution of work.

Strategic planners do not need on-line reporting of detailed facts, for they are concerned with the long-term; their use of computers is likely to be to run microeconomic and planning models, as aids in charting the firm's future work and prospects. At the level of management control, decisions are rarely required instantly, nor do they always depend on routine procedures that can be analysed and programmed in advance. It is for operational control that on-line reporting is of greatest value, for speedy responses are important here, and can be initiated by standard procedures. A well designed MIS provides each of these levels of management with the information and analyses it needs, and in the time-scale, form and degree of detail appropriate to its interests. It is a mistake to suppose that all levels need to know all about everything, and instantly.

9.1.4 *Shared systems.* In a sense every MIS is a shared system, for managers in the separate departments of a firm – accountants, personnel, sales, production – refer to the same database, and use programs from the same suite. But, there are a few examples of systems in which the sharers do not belong to the same organization, although they are related by a common interest. One such is the LACES computer which is used at London airport to process data related to the importation

164

and customs clearance of air freight. This computer is programmed and operated by the Post Office purely as a commercial
enterprise, and through remote terminals it provides a 24-hours-
a-week, service to H.M. Customs, the airlines and about 100
freight importing agents. (See Appendix 2.)

The airlines enter data about the arrival of individual
parcels, and their locations in the cargo sheds; H.M. Customs
use the computer to assess duty payments and to issue instructions about examinations and clearances; and the agents use it
to obtain information which assists them to detect the arrival
and note the clearance of their clients' consignments. LACES
provides an example of an on-line computer shared by users need-
ing the same kind of services and information, but who are in
fierce competition with each other; the confidentiality of their
information is protected by employing an independent, disinter-
ested party to operate the computer, and by the design of the
system. Each remote terminal operator has his own coded plastic
card which identifies him as a legitimate user of that particular terminal, and for certain specific purposes. Without the
proper card no information can be gained, and even with it the
only information available at the terminal is whatever that user
has been authorized to see.

Shared business services are also operated for information
related to stocks, shares and bonds, and for credit card auth-
orization; and we can expect to see a considerable expansion of
them as a means of communication and coordination between firms
with a common interest. In their design the virtual machine and
virtual storage concepts will be universal.

9.1.5 *Some consequences.* By discussing the consequences of computing in commerce in terms of MIS it is not intended to imply
that less-integrated uses are unimportant. That would be foolish indeed, for isolated systems have dominated business men's

use of computers, and they still constitute the major part. Nevertheless, MIS point the way ahead, and seem likely to have the more significant consequences.

The first of these consequences concerns the managers themselves. MIS tend to be designed by experts in computing rather than by managers working in the business; hence, there is a communications — and a generation — gap between the young, theoretical computer hawks, and the older, pragmatic managerial doves. As a result, many managers have felt themselves to be threatened, rather than helped, by the system. They may also be driven by it at a faster rate than they can sustain. We noted in chapter 8 that designers may not welcome being kept continuously at their peak of creativity; and managers also may not enjoy the highly concentrated information and decision processes which the system imposes, for they have been accustomed to large amounts of mental roughage, and a more relaxed pace of decision making. We may not reap the full crop of benefits from MIS until we have formally trained more business men in the 'management sciences', and this race of polymaths, philosopher-kings, has taken over from those who have acquired management as a craft skill rather than learned it as a science.

As a consequence of this change of background, management will become more explicitly rational, disciplined and systematic which will be fine provided we recall that information and calculation are not enough. A firm is *not* an impersonal cybernetic system, it is a social system in which considerations of power and status play an important part; where men are moved by charisma, initiative, ambition, jealousy and drive as well as by the logic of events. This is particularly true of the upper echelons of management, where vital decisions are taken affecting the survival and growth of the firm. In the jargon of management science, these high-level decisions are often 'ill-structured': to put it more plainly, they are not entirely rational,

166

and cannot be formalized; they depend on judgement and experience rather than a programmable evaluation of facts and figures. To know the facts is not enough: the essence of successful administration consists in acting boldly, but wisely, on inadequate information; and for this, as the team's trainer sang in Damn Yankees, "You gotta have heart".

The management of large enterprises, and of government departments, is the subject of a continual debate between the advocates of centralization and those of decentralization. Centralization makes for tight control and close coordination of all the organization's activities; but it also tends to destroy local initiative, which leads to flexibility and lowers the morale of the local managers. Decentralization has the converse pros and cons. However, the use of a management information system resting on a common data base gives access to the same information for the local control of operations by managers in the field, as for central planning and coordination. Such a system is sketched in Fig. 9.2, which shows a common computer and data base available to all headquarters and field managers alike. The existence of a single data base does not necessarily mean that every manager would be given access to every item of data filed in it; a different virtual machine and virtual file can be defined for each manager, or for related groups of managers. But, the means do exist to provide complete equality of treatment of headquarters and the field, and it would be meaningless to describe the system either as centralized, or as decentralized; conceptually it is both, for the computer exercises a common, not a central, function. It is worth underlining this point: computer technology does not dictate any one form of organization, the choice is ours alone.

9.1.6 *Conclusion*. Computers are used in business to increase the effectiveness of management, and to reduce the heavy overhead cost of office work. Many commercial applications of

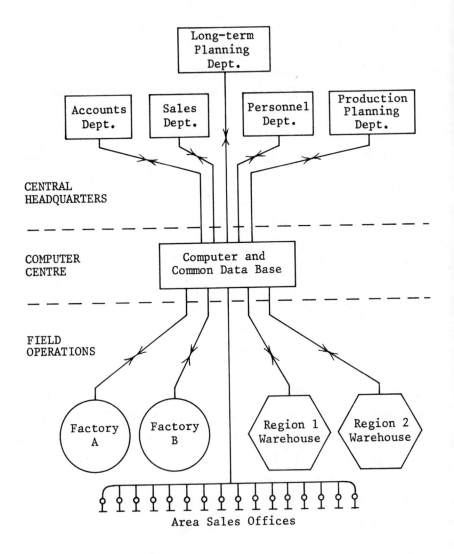

Fig. 9.2 Management information system with common data base.

168

computers have succeeded in both these objectives (see, for example, Appendix 2); but some have not. Where failures have occurred it has often been because:

(a) the computer was selected and installed without having established a sufficiently clear understanding of object-ives and priorities – perhaps because its purchase was handled superficially as a matter of prestige, or a re-sult of a blind enthusiasm;

(b) failures of communication between the computer experts and working managers have resulted in too much delegation of system design objectives and criteria to the experts;

(c) the computer has been indulgently regarded as the 'toy' of some parent department, without appreciating that its effects could not be confined within that department;

(d) some systems designers have sought to automate management by gross over-simplification, then as the size of the technical problems became apparent, have tried to use bigger machines and more systems work to buy their way out of a situation from which, by then, no one felt able to retreat.

As computer problems go, commercial arithmetic may appear to be simple, even trivial; but putting computers to effective use in business presents much more difficulty than the more advanced mathematics of scientific computing. It is, there-fore, a chastening thought that although it absorbs by far the greatest part of the time and money employed in computing, it has received the least attention from computer scientists. Perhaps Medawar was right to describe science as 'the art of the soluble'.

9.2 *Industry*

9.2.1 *The range of industrial use.* Industry's use of computers for office work is not really distinguishable from that of business, and raises no new problem; but computers are used also in a more direct association with the production process, notably in automatic control systems. Computer control is not of course, restricted to industry; we have already noted its use in traffic and weapon systems. Nor is automatic control the only direct industrial use, for we have noted the use of computers in design (CAD), and in the preparation of tapes for numerically-controlled machine tools – two techniques which have application to the mass production of clothing as well as to the manufacture of machine parts. Nevertheless, the inclusion of computers in the feed-back loops of automatic control systems is a most valuable technique, which offers many advantages in the continuous-process industries, and for the regulation of fast, complex machine operations.

9.2.2 *Automatic control of continuous processes.* We may take the refining of crude oil as an example of a continuous process. It is, indeed, particularly suitable for computer control because it is basically a rather simple process which is well understood, and which is capable of being described by a finite set of equations. The refinery is completely equipped with automatic measuring instruments to indicate quantities, compositions, rates of flow, pressures and temperatures at key points in the plant, and the readings of these instruments form part of the input data to the control computer. The other input data specify the composition and cost of the crude oil going in, and the proportions of the various refined products required to meet the current demand, or to optimize yield, or to maximize profits, or whatever other objective the firm wishes to set itself. The computer puts out signals that directly operate automatic switches and valves which regulate such factors as temperatures, pressures, flows, and the recycling of intermediate products. In this fashion the plant operating

onditions are set to produce the desired mix of products in
he most efficient way.

If the conditions were to remain steady, with everything
onstant, then the controls could be set and left, and the
omputer would offer little advantage. In practice, the raw
aterial and the output both change, and plant conditions vary
· for instance, a catalyst may age; and fixed settings of the
ontrols would soon cease to be optimal. The computer is pro-
rammed to interpret the control equations, and it continually
esets the controls to keep the performance of the plant with-
n specified limits. In some circumstances it is even possi-
le to make it change the settings experimentally in order to
ee whether this improves the result, and in this way to hunt
or and find the optimum setting for itself. As well as keep-
ng the plant operating at peak efficiency, the computer can
e programmed to detect potentially dangerous situations and
ake remedial action. What we have been saying about oil re-
ining very largely applies to other continuous-process plants,
or instance those for the manufacture of chemicals, paper or
ement.

.2.3 *Computer control of machinery.* The rising speeds of
anufacturing machinery means that its operation would be limi-
ed by human response times, particularly when the action to
e taken is a matter of thought and decision, rather than one
f reflex skill. A computer can be used to take over the mo-
ent-to-moment control, while accepting long-term direction
rom a human operator. For example, in a strip rolling mill
illets of red-hot steel weighing many tons are squeezed to a
inal thickness, and then cut into whatever lengths are re-
uired by customers. The strip moves through the mill at final
peeds of about 100 feet/sec., and the length produced from a
illet is not easy to predict, for it depends on the exact set-

171

tings of the rollers. It is, however, important to activate
the cutting shears at very precise instants in order to mini
mize the waste caused by leaving off-cuts of odd lengths. T
mill is instrumented and equipped with automatic controls op
erated by a computer which selects from a list of customers'
orders those which require a set of lengths that uses the ma
mum amount of the steel; and it operates the shears accordingly to cut the steel strip while it is on the move. The c
puter also controls the screw-down motors that regulate the
rolling pressure, in order to ensure a uniform thickness in
final strip.

Electrical generators provide another example of a comp
cated machine controlled by a computer. The starting-up fro
cold of a large generator is an elaborate procedure in which
100 or more operations have to be performed in the correct o
der, and at the proper times. The computer ensures that the
right sequence is meticulously followed, thus reducing wear
avoiding the risk of damage to a very expensive piece of equ
ment. The cost of providing and programming a small compute
can be covered if it prevents no more than one major failure
during the working life of a large generator. Again, the co
puter is used also to keep the generator operating at peak
efficiency, and for a large machine even a 1% increase in th
efficiency of fuel conversion can pay for the cost of its au
matic control in one year. A complex procedure is a feature
also of the launching of the large rockets used to put space
vehicles or communication satellites into orbit; and compute
control is an essential feature of the count-down that prece
ignition and take-off.

In the transport industry computer control is being app
ed to ships. The aim is to plan and follow a course which m
imizes fuel consumption, and the computer controls the engin
and the rudder in terms of data from the radar, radio naviga

172

ion aids, the compass and the log, and it corrects deviations rom the chosen course. The radar data are processed also to heck on the presence of other ships within range, and an alarm s raised when there is any risk of collision. For a tanker or container ship it has been estimated that the fuel saving in ne year's operation will pay the full cost of the computer ystem.

.2.4 *Needs, benefits & consequences of computer control.* For ndustrial use a computer system must provide a command and ontrol facade which is familiar enough and simple enough for he ordinary plant operators to use with confidence. The com- uter must be extremely reliable in continuous operation, with ery little time off for maintenance; it must be rugged enough ɔ accept the vibration, oil, moisture, dirt and heat of in- ustrial environments. Automatic control programs tend to have ɔre steps, more parallel paths and more checks than scienti- ic or business programs, and they are commonly written by the ltimate users - the plant engineers - rather than by special- st programmers. This arises in part because it is difficult ɔr a lay programmer to appreciate the technical subtleties of ıe process; and in part also because engineers are conserva- ive chaps. Up to now, most control programs have been written ı assembly languages, or even in machine code, in the inter- sts of efficiency, but high-level languages are coming into se.

The benefits of using computers in industrial control are:
ɪ) their ability to control high-speed processes;
ɔ) their capacity for dealing with complex situations in which the number of variables, and the nature of their interaction, are too much for unaided human thought to optimize;
ɔ) their condensation and simplification of the information presented to plant operators;

173

(d)   continuous maximization of profit for a given level and quality of output;

(e)   maximization of the output from a given supply of raw materials;

(f)   close control of product quality;

(g)   continuous surveillance of dangerous operations to ensu safety;

(h)   complete recording of plant variables, and of control actions, for subsequent analysis – either for post mort ems, or to increase our understanding of the process.

Computers offer to relieve men of dull, dirty and dangerous jobs – but, of course, they also offer to relieve men of job altogether.   Some indeed fear automation, or cybernation, as a threat to employment; and this topic is taken up in chapte 10.

9.3   *Bibliography*

A useful survey of the uses of computers in business, i cluding MIS, appears in:

(1)   *Computers, Managers and Society*, by Michael Rose.   Pen guin Books, 1969.

And, the problems of bringing them to profit are examined ir

(2)   *The Effective Use of Computers in Business*, by P.A. Los Cassell, 1969.

These problems are also outlined, with some of the consequer for managers, in:

(3)   *Using Computers, a Guide for the Manager*, by The Natior Computing Centre, 1971.

An analysis of the reasons why some commercial applications have failed to achieve the hoped for results is to be found

(4)   *The Effective Computer, A Management by Objectives Ap-proach*, by K. Gindley, and J. Humble.   McGraw Hill.

The industrial applications of computers tend to be dealt wi in articles scattered throughout the literature, and spread widely over the technical journals of the industries concerned. Control theory is a major subject in its own right, and has a highly specialist literature, which has little to do with computing as such. It follows that there is little that can be recommended to the general reader, for the detail of process control can be appreciated fully only by those who are already expert in the technicalities of the process concerned.

Examples 9

(9.1) Explain briefly the paradox that the simple arithmetic of commerce presents more trouble than the advanced mathematics of science, when it comes to programming them for a computer.

(9.2) Enthusiasts have claimed for some management information systems that they allow the Managing Director to have a VDU on his desk that can give him constantly updated information about the details of everything going on in his firm. Do you regard this as an appropriate design objective?

(9.3) It would be possible to couple the automatic control system of an oil refinery to a microeconomic model in order to extend its range to include:
- (a)   the operations of other refineries in the same firm;
- (b)   the distribution network for the firm's products;
- (c)   the control of the tanker fleet bringing the crude oil supply;
- (d)   the purchasing and pumping of crudes from alternative sources.

Discuss the implications of such an enlarged control system, and indicate any factors which could disturb its operation.

(9.4) Write notes, with reference to the use of computers, on one example each of:

(a) a completely cybernetic system;

(b) a process susceptible to partial control;

(c) an acybernetic situation.

(9.5) The headquarters' computer system of a large firm is designed as a database. Would you describe its function as data processing, or as communications?

(9.6) What circumstances favour the establishment of a shared computer system? Does such a system present any special problems?

(9.7) "In business organization computers have removed the need to choose between centralization and decentralization". Criticise and discuss this statement.

(9.8) Some business users have expressed keen disappointment about the results achieved by their computer systems. What precautions would you take to prevent this sorry state of affairs?

(9.9) In what circumstances is it better to teach a user to program his own work, rather than bring in a professiona programmer? Illustrate your answer with reference to

(a) scientific calculation;

(b) commercial data processing;

(c) automatic control systems.

(9.10) List the benefits offered by the use of computers for the automatic control of industrial machines and process

10 · Computers, government and society in a democracy

10.1 *Computers and the government*

The government's use of computers is not essentially different from that of business and industry. They hold records and keep accounts for civil servants; government statisticians and economists tabulate, analyse and drive models. Government scientists calculate; engineers in both local and central government apply the techniques of CAD; and computers are used for automatic control in the government's workshops and defence services.

There are, however, some important respects in which the government's use of computers does raise special problems. First, in dealing with affairs on a national scale the sheer size of the files makes them troublesomely large for the ordinary run of commercial equipment. Second, some government files contain confidential information about named men and women. Both problems are exemplified by the social security and taxation files. These two problems are quite different in character: the first is technical and economic, and open to rational solution as technical development proceeds; the second is ethical and political, and likely to prove very difficult to resolve. In the rest of this chapter we shall not be concerned with the detail of the more straightforward applications of computers to government business, for they raise no really new problems. We shall concentrate on some of the social and political implications of the widening use of computers.

The government's relation to computing is multidimensional, thus it is:

(a)   a major user, especially of the largest systems, and thu interested in operating efficiency and economy;

(b)   concerned about the effects of using computers on the productivity of industry and the level of employment;

(c)   broadly responsible for at least some of the conditions that determine the prosperity of its industry – including its computer hardware and software industries;

(d)   a major sponsor of computer R & D, in the universities and elsewhere;

(e)   interested in the effects – economic, industrial and military – of importing large quantities of computer equipment;

(f)   responsible, as banker and regulator, for the telecommunications authority which supplies the transmission link that carry computer data;

(g)   the guardian of the personal liberties of its citizens.

It is only to be expected that these roles will occasionally conflict.

10.2 *Computers and personal privacy*

It is the increasing use of computers to keep files of personal data about named men and women that is raising the issue of an individual's right to privacy. There is in this a conflict between the needs of the state and the rights of the individual. Any government that is actively concerned about the welfare of its citizens must have information about their needs and circumstances; it requires information also to ensure equity in the taxes it levies to pay for the services it provides. Some private businesses require us to disclose confidential personal data if we wish to use their services, the obvious examples are those concerned with credit and insurance.

178

Privacy is a vague concept, and one that varies with time and circumstances, and it is, of course, affected by much wider considerations than the use of computers. In computer files, however, it relates to an individual's right to control the collection and use of information about himself – to be able, at least, to participate in deciding what data shall be collected, and for what purpose. In Britain, there is no general right to privacy; indeed, it would clash with the right to know which is a part of the price we pay for living in a welfare-conscious democracy. The collection, filing and use of personal information was going on long before the computer age, so the problem of privacy is no new one: what the use of computers has done is to make it easier and cheaper to store and recover much larger volumes of data, and to provide remote access to them. It has also transferred the immediate custody of the data to technicians whose contacts with those who use the data are tenuous, and focussed on questions of efficiency and cost rather than of ethics and political rights. As U.S. Justice Louis Brandeis said in 1928, long before computers: "The greatest dangers to liberty lurk in insidious encroachments by men of zeal, well meaning but without understanding".

Again, there have been moves to apply the common data base concept to the pooling of personal information between different government departments, thus constituting what has been called a *databank*; and this could lead to data supplied for one purpose being applied to others in ways that might injure the individual concerned. Certainly, unless specific technical or administrative precautions were taken, personal records would become much more widely available, both within the department that collected them, and inside others that happened to be connected to the same databank. In this fashion, although the use of computers introduces no new principle, it does remove the protection which has, all unconsciously, been provided by the relative inaccessibility and inefficiency of manuscript files, and by their diffusion over many separate offices. The development of databanks is likely to be promoted by economic arguments which favour the use of large machines, and the consolidation of records into a single copy; and by the operational argument that when records are kept in one place, and in a large and efficient centre, they are more likely to be accurat up-to-date and comprehensive. It is important to note that th significant fact is not the keeping of the records in one computer centre, but in one virtual file; for, given a common reference number and good data communications, the contents of the virtual file could be spread over a number of physically separate centres and still operate effectively as a single database.

We have touched on databanks in a government context, but extensive files of personal data are also held commercially, particularly for credit control. Our lives are a kind of pape chase in which we leave an ever-lengthening trail of records behind us. Thus, facts about ourselves, our property, our activities and our movements are likely to appear in files kept for such varied purposes as: banking, the census, credit card payments (including hotels and travel), street and telephone directories, educational records, electoral rolls, insurance (life, car, valuables and house), licences (car, dog, gun and television), mailing lists, hospital and medical records, membership lists of societies, professional bodies and trades unions, military service records, police records, and for rates, taxes and social services.

The list grows longer every day. In some ways private files are more worrying than official ones, for they are less amenable to the pressure of public opinion or the complaints of MP's, nor is their existence always known to us.

The possible risks have provoked a considerable volume of public discussion, often characterized by heat rather than

180

light, and occasionally rising to a shrill, hysterical pitch when the computer's 'invasion of privacy' has been used as a convenient weapon to attack the advance of technology, or the extension of the welfare state[1,2,3,4]. Nevertheless, there seems to be general agreement that databanks are more likely to affect the individual than he is to be able to influence them, unless he is helped by establishing an explicit and detailed code of good practice. For example, it has been proposed in various places that an individual should have the right:

(a) to know for what specific purpose, and by whom, he is being asked to provide personal information, and which of the questions asked he is legally compelled to answer;

(b) to see a copy of his record in a databank, and be able to lodge an effective protest against errors, omissions, misrepresentations, and out-of-date or irrelevant material;

(c) to be provided with a list of all those who have obtained access to his record over a specified period;

(d) to be asked for his formal written consent before information that he has supplied for one stated purpose is used for a different, and clearly defined, purpose;

(e) to receive a copy of any transcript of his record which is made as a result of a legal process;

(f) to know the name of the one person who bears the full responsibility for the reliability and security of the databank or file;

(g) to be assured by independent expert inspection that adequate hardware, software, operational and physical security measures have been taken to protect the contents of the file against unauthorized use;

(h) to be told of the existence of all files that contain personal data about him;

(i) to apply to an 'Ombudsman' who has full power to investigate alleged irregularities - thus, Hesse in West Germany appointed a Data Protection Commissioner in 1973.

Such a code would not be effective unless it were made legally binding, and databank operators were licensed and inspected to ensure their compliance with its provisions. Inspection of a databank would, however, be a formidable task, for it would be extraordinarily difficult for a visiting official expert to establish that the computer was not doing anything unauthorized or that the records in its files contained nothing additional what his probing programs caused to be printed out: thus, cosmetic software could be devised to skip over parts of the record that someone wished to conceal. Again, the size and complexity of on-line executive and data processing programs, and their state of chronic amendment – often ahead of the documentation mean that it is impossible to check every path through a program, and it would be very hard to prove that some unscrupulous programmer had not included undocumented illegal routines that are triggered into action only when suitable coded parameters are entered at run time, for such routines would remain concealed throughout the official examination.

A number of attempts have been made to draft legislation to protect individual privacy, but they have foundered on the inherent conflict between the public's right to know, including the freedom of the press, and the individual's right not to be found out. Sweden was the first country to pass a Data Act (1973), and appoint a Data Inspection Board. We have here yet another example where the coming of the computer has sharpened up our perception of an old problem, forcing us to think more clearly than before about what it is – precisely – that we want to achieve.

10.3 *Computers and employment*

10.3.1 *Automation and productivity*. Productivity is an output input ratio which we use to measure the amount of some resource that is consumed in producing a unit of output. Most often, the resource is labour, and in this context increased product-

182

ivity tends to be used as a euphemism for the reduction of labour's contribution to unit production costs. Lower costs are essential in a country such as Britain which depends on a high volume of exports in increasingly competitive world markets, and so there is a considerable emphasis laid on productivity in the planning of new schemes. Experience shows that significant increases in productivity come from advances in technique rather than from increases of the worker's effort or skill; indeed it is usual for both of these to decrease.

Automation, including the use of computers, provides a substantial advance in technique, and automation projects are initiated, planned and launched by the management, not by the workers, in their ceaseless pursuit of productivity and economy. Normally, increased productivity means fewer jobs, unless the lower production cost can be used to stimulate an increased demand for the goods produced. However, there is not much evidence that the use of computers has so far produced any large-scale redundancy, although they have been used to check the growth of the labour force in some areas. They have, of course, created jobs in a new industry of substantial size, but these jobs have not been filled by those displaced by computers. Thus, the introduction of a computerized phototype-setting machine into one British newspaper reduced the composing room staff from 276 to 166, but it is most unlikely that the displaced printing staff entered the computer industry.

Automation reduces the number of man-hours needed to produce a unit of output, but it does not require this to be done by reducing the number of men employed rather than the number of hours they work. No law of nature or economics demands that men shall work for 40 hrs x 50 weeks x 45 years, and in the future many will have a much shorter working life than that. Some will welcome their increased leisure as an unmixed bless-

ing, but for many the empty hours will gape, as time to be
filled or killed as quickly and as painlessly as possible;
and, unfortunately, those most likely to be displaced by aut
mation are also those whose education has least prepared the
to enjoy the leisure that will be thrust upon them. Boredom
especially in the active young, could lead to 'delinquent' b
haviour which expresses the individual's frustration and re-
sentment of the society that has failed to make him feel tha
he has a valued, indeed unique, part to play in its life and
work.

10.3.2 *Computers and the unions.* The majority of the popula
tion is inherently sceptical of the benevolence of masters o
all kinds, including its governments; nor does it leap with
at the prospects of the increased productivity that should
follow the use of computers in business and industry, for th
suspect that their employer's prime motive is to reduce his
wage costs rather than to improve the lot of the working mar
They know also that automatic methods replace craft skills b
machine-minding, and thus for the great majority destroy the
interest and the challenge presented by their work.

For these reasons the trades unions are seeking to part
cipate in the planning of automation schemes, in the hope of
influencing the choice of objectives, and the selection of t
criteria which the designers will use. Systems analysts and
programmers tend to be rather self-sufficient experts engros
with technical efficiency and, because of their youth and th
background, they have, at best, only a second-hand acquainta
with the work and the workers that will have to live with th
systems they design. System design is heavily influenced by
the 'dictatorship of the optimum'; however, multiple optima
rarely to be achieved and, having little in common with othe
workers in their firm, the designers seek to please their en
ployers by concentrating on minimizing his costs and maximis

184

his benefits, leaving the human consequences to be what they may. For example, a computer with its programs is a very heavy capital investment which achieves its highest return when it is operated 7 days a week and 24 hours a day - the so-called 4-shift system which the staff and their unions dislike. Again, it is cheaper to make magnetic tape and disk stores that work in windowless, air-conditioned rooms rather than in an environment more pleasant for men and women; and so cost/benefit analyses dictate that their working conditions should conform to those that suit the machines. The unions hope that, by being consulted before plans and objectives are set in concrete, they will be able to persuade the designers to take account of human, social and environment factors, as well as costs and efficiency. But first they will have to convince their employers that they are not just Luddites, aiming to obstruct innovation and preserve jobs.

The ever-growing applications of computers, and their use as the sole means of performing functions that are vital to the economic health and survival of a firm, is greatly increasing the power of some trades unions to take damaging industrial action to further their own purposes. Thus, a 7-weeks strike of computer staff at three centres producing telephone bills cost the Post Office £23 millions in interest charges on the money it had to borrow to replace the revenue it was unable to collect until later. This strike was used to settle a claim over a wider range of work than computing, simply because office and computer staff happened to be members of the same union. Action by a few computer men and women was sufficient to force a settlement for a very much larger number of their associates, for because so small a proportion of the union's members was on strike they could have been supported indefinitely by a very modest levy on the rest.

This example illustrates a more general proposition, name-

ly that as computer systems take over more industrial, commercial and governmental functions, and as they are more closely knit together by data links, so the whole 'infra-structure'
of a nation will become more fragile and vulnerable to dis-
ruption by:

(a) trades unions taking industrial action;

(b) disgruntled ex-employees - programmers especially;

(c) citizens or consumer rights groups;

(d) industrial spies or saboteurs;

(e) mischievous computer 'phreaks';

(f) criminal action, or the threat of it;

(g) political activists - 'data hijacking'.

Because we appear to be moving steadily into a phase in which
democratic debate, and compliance with the established norms
of society, are being replaced by 'direct action', these possibilities may soon have to be taken into explicit account in
the planning and design of computer systems. Moreover, as
multi-national business and economic groupings continue to develop so the problems will rise to the international level,
and meet all the complications of differing legal systems and
commercial practices.

10.4 *Social responsibility and computing*

Few can doubt that computers have acquired a bad public
image; the press delights in headlining 'their' stupid mistakes, and ordinary men and women see them as the archetypal
product of that advanced industrial technology which they dislike and fear. As we have seen, these attitudes are not without foundation, for left to themselves computer system designers tend to produce systems which are dominated by technical
considerations, and remote, insensitive and coldly mechanical
in their impact on their 'slaves' and their 'victims' alike.
However, large corporations are now very concerned about their

186

public images, and take pains to be seen to be organizations worthy of public respect, and anxious to discharge their social duties and responsibilities. This concern provides us with an opportunity to extend the evaluation of alternative designs of computer systems to include social factors, in much the same way as concern for pollution and energy conservation have led to the methods of 'Technology Assessment' being used to estimate the total effects of a civil engineering project, or an industrial plant, on men and their environment.

In another field, as mini- and micro-computers become really cheap we can expect to see them expand into education, both at school and in the home. There are enormous opportunities for home education, which might begin by a stealthy building on our leisure interests - botany for gardeners, physics for photographers, and languages for the holiday traveller. It would, however, open up some alarming possibilities for mind-conditioning, which would be all the more effective by being self-inflicted and conveyed with the authority of a seemingly impartial and powerful machine. Again, such education would unfortunately tend to benefit those who needed it least, for the competent would become more so, and those who are less so would fall even further behind in the meritocratic stakes. Computer based information systems may also widen a similar split between the information-rich and the information-poor nations, thus exacerbating the conflict between the Western industrial nations and the under-developed third world. The use of computers may, indeed, prove to be socially divisive, even though the automated information network they make possible will tie the commercial-industrial complex more tightly together.

If our use of computers is to be socially responsible, then we must decide what social ends and priorities to use as counterweights to considerations of cost and efficiency. What do we want to achieve? An ever-growing mass production of consumer goods? The elimination of deprivation and poverty? Better amenities and an improved environment? This list coul be continued, but it is already long enough to suggest that i will take quite some time to establish even a minimum set of agreed aims and criteria. Once again, the introduction of tl computer has not of itself raised any new issue, but it has increased the urgency of dealing with some old ones; and it i forcing us to think much more clearly and precisely than we ever did before about exactly what it is we want to do.

10.5 *Computers and democracy*

Democracy is far from being an easy concept to define, although we all know what we mean by 'undemocratic': the term is used below to refer to the type of political system that i to be found in the representative democracies of the Western world. One feature of these systems is the two-way exchange of views between the government and the governed, including those of the governed who have organized themselves into groups to promote policies contrary to those of the govern-ment, but which are nonetheless allowed free access to the sources of information and the organs of persuasion.

We now have the technical means to intensify this demo-cratic dialogue, and some have proposed that push-button vot-ing and on-line computers should be used to settle matters of policy by national referenda. This at first appears to be a praiseworthy attempt to re-establish democracy in its purest Athenian form, but reflection suggests some troublesome side-effects. Thus, in practice very few voters would be prepared to spare the time and effort needed to brief themselves ade-quately on the complex issues that face governments today. Many, perhaps most, would push their voting buttons after but little thought, doing so on impulse or on the basis of their most recent exposure to indoctrination. The result would thus depend less on rational deliberation by the whole body politic than on mindless guesswork, or the manipulations of plausible demagogues. Such a system would be an instant electronic populism, not a responsible, participant democracy. On its surface the democratic process seems to be a matter of counting heads, but its essence is the peaceful reconciliation of conflicting interests, and the achievement of pragmatic compromises and accommodations.

Computer techniques are also being brought into the dialogue through their use in opinion polling, and these polls could have two disturbing effects on the democratic scene. First, they may distort the voting pattern in elections, either by persuading the lazy that their party is so certain to win that they need not bother to vote; or by attracting the fickleminded to leap onto the winning bandwagon. Second, they could be used to conduct a market survey of what policies would be most popular, and thus to erect a party platform not on political principles but on what will attract the most votes at the time. Why should this be wrong? First, because people are usually asked to give on-the-spot responses to market surveys, with no opportunity to give the questions adequate consideration; second, because the answers obtained are greatly influenced by the nature and the exact wording of the questions asked; and third, because there is no reason to suppose that the result would reflect anything more than mere opportunism.

The questions of policy faced by democratic governments are becoming more and more complex and technical, and thus more and more beyond the reach of unassisted common sense. Few electors have the inclination to devote the time needed to muster the facts, or the capacity needed to master the techniques required to reach soundly-based conclusions. In many instances the circumstances are so complex that computer simulation and modelling are the only line of attack. How

nice it would be, some say, if we were to use system dynamics
econometric modelling, planned programming and budgeting, and
other management science techniques to steer our governments
towards better decisions. Often, however, we have neither
enough data, not adequate theories; and we are not likely to
agree about the meaning of 'better' in this context.

Again, the modelling method of reaching decisions would
be largely beyond the comprehension of the average elector,
and of his elected representative also. When the modelling
was competent and honest how could we reasonably challenge it
results, for these would have been reached by powerful techniques backed by infallible, incorruptible and impartial mach
ines? But, if we could not challenge, would we not soon beco
those ciphers in cyberland that Olof Johanneson portrays so
well in his vision of life in a "Total Freedom Democracy"?[5].
The consequence could only be to add to the alienation of the
electorate, by diminishing still further our already modest
sense of participation in the democratic process. Effective
political power would then pass into the hands of the model
builders, for only they would understand precisely how the
models worked, what presumptions were built into them, and
what data they processed. This would be a quite unacceptable
creation of a technical elite; and they, or their paymasters,
would be exposed to the risk of mistaking their methodology
for metaphysics - of concluding that because it is convenient
to analyse some phenomenon in a certain way, that this is al
the way in which that part of the world really works. Such a
premature, and immature, conclusion that they had attained to
absolute truth might persuade them to compel the obedience of
any who disagreed - purely in their own long-term interests,
course. Another consequence of modelling would be to draw to
gether the private and public sectors of the economy as each
came to use the same data, apply the same programs to its ana

lysis, and employ the same cost/benefit criteria to evaluate the results. It does not follow that democracy would be advanced if these two sectors were to fuse and precipitate us into a managerial state.

The tone of this section has been sombre, but computers are not essentially undemocratic. What they do depends on what we order them to perform, and like mirrors they reflect the characteristics of those who use them; but they are magnifying mirrors, which enlarge our blemishes as well as our excellences. They can make good men better, but they also make bad men worse; and this is true whether we are speaking of competence or morals.

As their use continues to extend throughout business and industry computers will affect us as workers, as consumers, and by adding to our leisure. In such government services as health, education, welfare and taxation they will modify our interaction with the state. As they enter the information network, and are used for news, culture and entertainment, our minds will be enlarged, or massaged. It is by permeating and influencing all our activities that computers will first, and most profoundly, affect democracy, rather than by any direct application to the political process itself. We cannot reasonably doubt that democracy will cope with the computer; it may bend and creak, but it will not break. As Fisher Ames put it, "Democracy is like a raft. It never sinks, but, damn it, your feet are always in the water".

10.6 *Conclusion*

The social consequences of using computers will depend on how fast they are introduced, for we are still at the beginning. Experience so far suggests that we will have time to adjust our habits, and adapt our institutions. The process may not be comfortable, but it is inescapable, and a necessary phase of our development: to opt out because we are too frightened to use our own creations would be to be less than human.[8,9]

10.7 *Bibliography*

The subject of privacy and the computer has a most voluminous literature. It has been discussed ad nauseam in the press, conferences have been held, books have been written and draft legislation prepared. A much quoted book on surveillance generally is:

(1) *Privacy and Freedom*, by Alan F. Westin. Athaneum, New York, 1967.

A conference entitled 'Workshop on the Data Bank Society' was held in London in 1970, and is fully reported in:

(2) *Privacy, Computers and You*, ed. B.C. Rowe. National Computing Centre, 1972.

This book includes a bibliography of more than 120 references. In the USA the subject has been even more volubly discussed than in Europe, and a good summary of American thinking is to be found in the Report of the Secretary's Advisory Committee on Automated Personal Data Systems:

(3) *Records, Computers and the Rights of Citizens*. U.S. Department of Health, Education and Welfare, 1973.

This report has a 33 page bibliography. There is also a British government report:

(4) *Report of the Committee on Privacy*, by K. Younger, Chairman. H.M.S.O., 1972.

The effects of computers on society have been the subject of widespread speculation. A perceptive and witty account of a cybernetic utopia appears in:

(5) *The Great Computer*, by Olof Johanneson (Hannes Alfven) Gollancz, 1968.

And less futuristic treatments are given in:

(6) *The Computerised Society*, by J. Martin and A.R.D. Norman. Penguin Books, 1973.

And:

(7) *Computers and the Year 2000.* National Computing Centre, 1972.

The possible effects on men and women is treated by a pioneer of cybernetics in:

(8) *The Human Use of Human Beings. Cybernetics and Society,* by Norbert Wiener. Sphere Books, 1968.

And in:

(9) *Future Shock,* by Alvin Toffler. Pan Books, 1970.

Examples 10

(10.1) Discuss the advantages to a country of having the manufacture of computers established within its own borders. Does it matter if this manufacture is foreign owned?

(10.2) "Those who fear the invasion of privacy by computers are concerned about the possibility of injustice rather than the disclosure of personal information". Discuss.

(10.3) What items would you like to be included in the code of good practice for the keeping of personal records in computer files, in addition to those listed in par. 10.2?

(10.4) Discuss the limitations on total rationality in politics.

(10.5) Outline the role of government in relation to the development, manufacture and use of computers in its country.

(10.6) Do you consider that the establishment of databanks containing identifiable personal information constitutes a threat to the individual? Which could offer the greater risk, public databanks or private ones?

(10.7) "The other side of the productivity coin is enforced leisure". Discuss.

(10.8) If you were a trade union leader what aspects of the development of computing would you wish to study?

(10.9) Do you agree that computer assisted referenda would be the acme of democracy?

(10.10) The complex policy decisions faced by modern governments can be satisfactorily reached only with the support of computer modelling; but the use of this technique
removes the bases of decision ever further from the comprehension of the ordinary voter. How would you resolve this dilemma?

Appendix 1 · Notes on the solutions to the examples

(1.1)   (a)   4 bytes = 32 bits,   (b)   2 bytes = 16 bits
         (c)   1111100011011 = 13 bits.

(1.2)   (a)   0.69632, 05   ;   0.10001 , 10001
         (b)   0.1024 , 04   ;   0.10000 , 01011
         (c)   0.6250 , −01   ;   0.10000 , −00011

(1.3)   (a)   As three separate fields of 2,2 and 3 digits,
                for the hours, minutes and seconds respect-
                ively, thus avoiding conversion and allowing
                direct output for reproduction.
         (b)   As so many tenths of a second, expressed in
                binary for easy arithmetic.
(1.4)   Mantissa 16 bits;   Exponent 8 bits.
         (a)   Multiply the mantissas, add the exponents,
                re-normalize.
         (b)   Convert to fixed-point representation, add,
                re-convert.
(1.5) See par. 1.4 and 1.7
(1.6) Differences of make, model, configuration, and of main-
       tenance adjustment by the service engineers. Different
       suppliers of data media, e.g. cards, tapes or disks.
       Different editions of the manufacturers control soft-
       ware (operating system, see index). Inadequate docu-
       mentation of operating instructions, especially of re-
       start and recovery procedures required when hardware,
       software or program faults or data errors occur.

(1.7)   See par. 1.9

In Fig. 1.2 *Conditional Jumps* at the tests for:
Last Transaction?, Quantity Less or Greater?,
N = Total number of records?, Transaction and record
Codes Same or Different?, Transaction a Sale or De-
livery? *Unconditional Jumps* at Return to Read Next
Transaction, Return to Read Nth Record.

(1.8)   (a)   The 'Last Transaction?' test would probably fail,
unless the character used to indicate this happened to be the same on both tapes. Then, the com
parison of transaction and record item codes would
probably hang up, for either the codes would be of
quite different kinds making comparison impossible
if, by ill-chance, they happened to be similar it
is unlikely that a match would be found, and the
computer would endlessly traverse the 'Read Next
Stock File Record - Compare Codes' cycle thus entering a 'pathological loop' condition, which woul
soon become apparent because the transaction tape
would not advance.

(b)   The Stock File would be incorrectly up-dated once
again in terms of the old transactions which had
already been taken into account, a month previousl
when the out-of-date tape was run at its proper
time. This situation can be avoided by recording
its 'Next Run Date' at the start of the tape, and
including preliminary instructions in the program
to check this date against 'Today's Date' before
proceeding, and Jump to inform the operator if the
dates do not agree.

(1.9)   See par. 1.9

Note, however, that only those who wrote the program
fully understand what decisions and criteria it include

It is hardly possible for a layman (and not at all easy for another programmer) to satisfy himself that these are doing what, and only what, they are supposed to be doing. Again, cumulative amendment and expansion of the program may increase this uncertainty, and if these are inadequately documented (and documentation costs time, trouble and money) then eventually no one will know in complete detail what the program does. Complacency and indolence prompt us to accept a program that works, without undertaking the arduous task of checking it.

(1.10) See par. 1.9 for the first part, and for (a).

(b) Modification of the Function Part is less common; it could be used in a program corresponding to the flow chart of Fig. 1.2 after the 'Transaction Sale or Delivery'? test to modify the next operation from Add to Subtract according as the test showed the transaction to be a delivery or a sale. It is, however, much more usual to Jump to either an Add or to a Subtract instruction.

(2.1) See par. 2.2 (a) to (f).

Query relevance of Sex (equal pay?), marital status, place of birth, religion. Missing data: position on basic pay scale, income tax code, total tax paid to date, hours worked, overtime, special allowances (e.g. for skills), regular deductions (e.g. for pension, insurance, charities, etc.).

(2.2) See par. 2.3

(2.3) (a) 1 byte (character) per row = 1.55 char/cm^2 = 12.4 bit/cm^2.

(b) 80 char./card = 0.52 char/cm^2 = 4.15 bit/cm^2.

(c) 960 bits/card = 6.22 bit/cm^2.

(d) 3 lines x 62 char. = 6.1 char/cm^2 = 48.8 bit/cm^2.

(e) 1 byte per row (the 9th track records a check bit
$226 \text{ char/cm}^2 = 2130 \text{ bit/cm}^2$.

(2.4)

		TIME	
		Bible	500 bits Message
(a)	Teleprinter	258 hours	12 seconds
(b)	Telephone dict-ation.	107 hours	about 5 sec; (equivalent).
(c)	1st Class Post	24 hours	24 hours
(d)	Courier	3 hours	3 hours
(e)	5 k bit/sec. Datel	1.9 hours	0.1 second
(f)	48 k bit/sec. Datel	0.2 hour	0.01 second

Telecommunications good for short, slow for long,
messages.

(2.5)   – Dot or Bar Codes, see par. 2.3
      – Mark Sensing or Scanning, see par. 2.4
      – Data Capture at Source, see par. 2.7
      – Keyboard Input, see par. 2.5

(2.6)   See par. 1.3 and 2.5; see also 3.4.2.

(2.7)   See par. 2.5 and 2.10.

(2.8)   See par. 2.5 (iii) N.B. also: the use of paper of
standard size, and quality suitable for mechanical hand
ling; the need to avoid dirt, over-printing or carelessly
corrected errors (imperfect erasure); the importance
of correct and uniform line spacing; clear impression
required, i.e. uniform key pressure, type hammers clean
(no smudging) and ribbon not worn (impression not pale)
and of correct colour (e.g. black not blue or red) to
suit the optics.

(2.9)   See par. 2.7.
      Advantages: human transcription errors avoided, time an

cost savings.

Disadvantages: inflexible, amount of data restricted, limited opportunity to recheck – e.g. that the wrong tag has been sent.

(2.10) See par. 2.6

(3.1)   See par. 3.4.2. Note that the dictionary does not have to cope with names, including prefixes such as Mac or Mc., Saint or St. etc., with trade names including numbers, idiosyncratic arrangements of initials and forenames, alpha-numeric addresses, etc.

(3.2)   See par. 3.4.2

    (a)   punched cards too bulky, too slow, prone to loss of a card and to loss of sequence,

    (b)   this program would be lost on a 2400 ft reel of tape, for it would occupy only an inch or two; but it would fit conveniently into about 20 cards.

(3.3)   (a)   See par. 3.3. The contents can be compact; the data are mostly numerical, and are compiled and checked by specialist operators; are re-copied each time the file is up-dated; the file is used within a single firm and can be economically designed for its specific functions.

    (b)   See par. 3.4.1. The contents are discursive, mostly non-numerical; are compiled by various medical staff in different hospitals and surgeries; are rarely amended, but continually added to; have to last at least for the patient's lifetime (up to 100 years), and be suitable for confidential use on a national scale.

(3.4)   Main problem: extremely wide range of alphabets – occasionally mixed within one line of print, very diverse layouts, high standard of accuracy and print quality required; all of these make printing and checking difficult. Alternative: graphical output display, or microfilm, produced by cathode-ray tube character genenerator – see par. 3.7.4 and 3.7.7.

(3.5)   See par. 3.4.1

(3.6)   See par. 3.3

   (a) *Tapes*: payroll record files; regular billing file national files that are too large to be kept on today's disks.

   (b) *Disks*: airline seat-reservation files; motor insurance files; bank account (ledgers); – to allow on-demand interrogation to check availability, coverage or credit.

(3.7)   See par. 3.2.2, 3.2.3, 3.4.1, 3.4.2

   Logical Elements: Bit, Character, Field, Record, File Database.

   Technical Elements: Bit, Byte, Word, Block (or Sector) Reel (or Disk).

(3.8)   See par. 3.2.2

   Interblock Gap equivalent to 640 bytes

   (a) Block Size: 1024 bytes:
      Tape Utilization $1024/(1024 + 640)$ i.e. 62%
      Data transfer rate = $0.62 \times 160 = 99$ k bytes/sec.

   (b) Block Size: 4096 bytes:
      Tape Utilization $4096/(4096 + 640)$ i.e. 87%
      Data transfer rate = $0.87 \times 160 = 139$ k bytes/sec

(3.9)   See par. 3.2.3, 3.4.2

(3.10) (i) Design A. Effective speed 3000 l.p.m.
       Design B. Effective speed 1500 l.p.m.

   (ii) Design A. Effective speed $2/10 \times 3000 = 600$ l.p.m
        Design B. The 8 blank lines are skipped in the time it would take to print 2 lines; hence:
        Effective speed $2/4 \times 1500 = 750$ l.p.m

(iii) Design A.   Has to print 4 times;
                  hence:
                  Effective speed 1/4 x 600 = 150 l.p.m.
       Design B.   1+3 Carbon copies are possible by using
                  a '4-part set' of stationery,
                  hence:
                  Effective speed remains at 750 l.p.m.

(4.1)   *ALGOL*

```
begin
comment Vieta Pi;
real A,P,N;
integer count;
read N;
A:=0;   P:=1;   count:=0;
for count:= count + 1  while count < N do
    begin
    A:= sqrt(2+A);
    P:= PxA/2;
    end;
print (2/P);
end
```

(4.2)   Problems arise from the need to

(a)   include a very comprehensive alphabet covering
        mathematical, statistical, etc. signs and sym-
        bols

(b)   incorporate a wide range of procedures to cope
        with commercial files, mathematical and graphic
        design routines, process control loops etc.

(c)   strike different balances between ease of writ-
        ing the source program by non-specialists, and
        efficiency in the compiled object program, say,
        for short ephemeral scientific work and long
        automatic control programs.

A catch-all language would require a large complex compiler program, which implies a lot of processing and a large main store. On any one occasion much of the compiler and store would not be needed, and this inefficiency would lead to the use of specialist sub-sets of the language, e.g. for mathematics. Moreover, such subsets would be simpler to learn, remember and use effectively, by non-specialists programming only occasionally. If subsets, then the case for a universal language is weakened.

(4.3)   (a)   Job Requirement Specification, see par. 4.4.1

       (b)   Systems Definition, see par. 4.4.2

       (c)   Description of modules, programs and suites, see par. 4.4.5

       (d)   Program Maintenance, see 4.4.6

Cobol program insufficient because it would not describe what was required to be done, only what had been done; not the problem, only one solution. Nor would it reveal the thinking that led to that particular solution, and it is valuable to know this when amending or extending somebody else's program - i.e. when program maintenance is needed and the original programmer is no longer available.

(4.4)   English text input conversion to binary code is a simple replacement of letters etc. of a limited alphabet by their binary code equivalents, character by character in a 1-for-1 substitution.

Compilation of Cobol involves recognising the meanings of each of a virtually unlimited range of statements written in a standard form, generating the corresponding set of instructions, checking for and rejecting syntactical errors, allocating space in the main store for variables and constants, and so on. See par. 4.4.4

(4.5) See par. 4.2

    (a) Faulty numerical analysis.

       Errors or imprudent approximations in the mathematics.

    (b) Logical Errors.

       Instructions do not correspond to the numerical analyst's specification.

    (c) Syntactical Errors.

       Instructions incorrectly expressed.

    (d) Transcription Errors.

       Errors in copying or inputing the program.

    (e) Inappropriate Data.

       Irrelevant, incorrect or insufficiently precise.

(4.6) O & M. See par. 4.4.1

    Systems Analyst, see par. 4.4.1, 4.4.2

    Senior Programmer, see par. 4.4.3

    Coders, see par. 4.4.4

(4.7) See par. 4.4.4

    The examples are all drawn from an instruction in the Algol program in (4.1) above

    The correct form is A := sqrt(2+A);

    Logical Error   A := sqrt(2+sqrt(A));

    Syntactical Error   A := sqrt(2+A) ;

    Transcription Error A := sqtt(2+A);

(4.8) See par. 4.4.2

    Prevention: ensure that experience is brought to the aid of intelligence, either by training working managers in Systems Analysis; or by effectively organized mixed teams of systems analysts and managers.

(4.9) See par. 4.4.3, 4.4.4

(4.10) See par. 4.3

(5.1) (i) (a) Technological obsolescence before wear-out; an economic case for replacement can usually be made after 5 years of use.

        (b)   Reduced pressure on program efficiency; it is often cheaper to transfer the program to a newer (faster) machine than to revise and streamline it.

    (ii)   Commercial work involves large volumes of input and output, and the speeds of input, output and backing store peripherals have not increased by so large a factor. And, the times required by operators to change tapes, disks or printer paper have not decreased. Moreover, the time of a faster machine has often to be shared by multiprogramming – in order to match its peripherals – and this wastes time in housekeeping.

(5.2) – One data stream commonly goes with one of everything else.

       – Several concurrent streams of data, and one program (or suite) are found when a common function is performed for several users, e.g. airline seat reservation.

       – Several data streams and multiprogramming typify online, real time use; e.g. a multiaccess system for a university.

       – Increasing the number of separate store units increase speed and reliability, as does more processors; this last also allows specialized processors to be used (see par. 5.1.6).

(5.3) See par. 5.1.3, 5.1.4, 5.2.2

(5.4) *Costs*

     Hardware: initial, foreseeable extensions.

     Accommodation: room, false flooring, air conditionin special power supplies.

     Operating: staff, power, consumable stores, main tenance.

Software:	manufacturer's software, initial programs, programming maintenance.
Performance	point-by-point comparison with user's own specification, others' experience of serviceability.
Delivery	date, and achievement for others, availability of machine for program development before delivery.

Many of these factors can enter a cost comparison extended to the end of the working life of each machine; and it is usual to discount all costs to the present date in order to allow for different patterns of expenditure, e.g. lower initial cost but higher annual maintenance. Credit may be taken for any surplus work capacity, provided this can be used or sold.

User convenience covers many 'unquantifiable benefits', but others may be costed and compared, thus:

(a) extra programming time or talent needed for machines difficult to program, or limited in facilities,

(b) cost of extra capacity needed to avoid unpopular three-shift working,

(c) cost of conversational real-time facilities, and of extra capacity needed to give quicker response.

(5.5) See par. 5.3

(5.6) See par. 5.1.5
Microprograms are usually written by the manufacturer's design team.

(5.7) See par. 5.1.4
Users in a system operating several programs concurrently; especially when which programs run together varies according to users' needs, as these happen to arise; rather than being set by a pre-planned schedule.

(5.8) See par. 5.1.5

      (a)   Miniaturization, parallel CPU's, pipelining.

      (b)   Improved numerical or systems analysis that break the problem down into smaller self-contained frag ments. Substituting thought and insight for brut force calculation wherever possible.

(5.9) See par. 5.2.1

To avoid the need to store multiple copies of a progra that is being run by several independent users at the same time.

(5.10) See par. 5.1.7

      (i)   Channel switching: setting-up and clearing-down times incurred once only for the whole message; a no intermediate storage and processing delays and costs.

      (ii) Packet switching: for flexibility, and to cope ec nomically with a fluctuating load.

      (iii) Store-and-forward: accumulate data by day, and transmit in bulk by night when the rates are re- duced.

(6.1) *PRO* Can buy: only what is required, from alternative (cheaper) suppliers, extra facilities offered by competing suppliers.

      CON problems of choosing facilities and suppliers; ha ware manufacturer may not accept responsibility f poor performance with other's software; alternati supplier's software for a new machine may be held up; explicit payment required for software improv ments.

      (a)   More freedom as manufacturer

         (i)   has less need to limit his software develop- ment costs.

         (ii) can handicap the independent software suppli by changing it,

         (iii) can obsolete his old software.

(b)   Hamper standardization as alternative suppliers search for competitive advantages.

(6.2)   *Problems*; competing demands leading to processing delays; time sharing arrangements interrupting a program before it has completed its use of a subroutine; subroutine modified by a program in execution.

        Solution: Competition handled by Operating System, which assigns priorities and protects programs from each other's actions; time sharing designed to allow completion of a subroutine once started; all subroutines written as pure procedures (see par. 5.2.1).

(6.3)   In Computer Aided Design for Engineers

        Procedure Oriented Language will be mainly designed to help the writing of programs to plot numerical data, to draw standard elements, e.g. straight lines, circles, ellipses etc., and to keep data lists specifying drawn shapes, and to manipulate these algebraically in order to change the plotting axes or scales.

        Problem Oriented Language will be designed to simplify programming the manipulation of drawn shapes by the inclusion of macros to reposition, re-scale, delete, recall, rotate the whole or parts of drawings; and to calculate areas, volumes, weights, strengths, etc.

(6.4)   *FORTRAN* $Y**2$ rather than y^2 because the average computer input keyboard has only capital letters, and no provision for entering small raised indices. $4*Z$ rather than $4z$ because it is desirable to have a positive indication that 4 and z are to be multiplied, and x may be needed to represent another quantity.

COBOL   Capitals rather than mixed upper and lower
             case letters, as for Fortran. NETPAY rather
             than NET PAY to indicate that it is the name
             of one quantity and not the names of two.

(6.5)   See par. 6.2.1
        Example: subroutine for computing square roots include
                  within a larger mathematical subroutine, e.g.
                  for solving quadratic equations.

        Macros: See par. 6.3.3

(6.6)   See par. 6.2.2 and manufacturer's literature.

(6.7)   See par. 6.2.3, 6.3.2, 6.3.4

(6.8)   See par. 6.4
        Varieties: e.g. batch, real-time, tape-based, disk-
                    based, single or multi-processor.

(6.9)   Growth by a factor of ten every 5 years would soon:
        (a)   raise the cost and effort of production to un-
              acceptable levels;
        (b)   make validation virtually impossible;
        (c)   create severe storage problems in computer systems

(6.10) See par. 6.6
        Users may be tempted to postpone the re-writing of the
        old machine's programs; these may run faster when simu-
        lated on the new machine but the simulation housekeepin
        overhead wastes much of the new machine's time, and
        frustrates the user's expectations of improved efficien
        and economy.

(7.1)   Qualitative judgements are codified for processing, e.g
        by ranking. Thus, in personnel work, 'initiative' migh
        be rated:
        Code 5- Exceptional;   4- Above average;   3- Average;
             2- Below average;   1- Abysmal.
        Individuals could then be sorted and grouped in terms o
        these codes.

Difficulties; The ranking scale is very coarse, but
finer division would be meaningless, for
different assessors will make their subjective judgements with differing degrees
of realism. Again, the number codes are
'labels' not 'quantities', and we have to
remember not to combine them with others
in arithmetical processing. Some qualitative factors are too complex for a single
ranking, but multiple coding exacerbates
the problems.

(7.2) If the objective is better/cheaper translations, it is
simpler/quicker to train men and women. But machine
translation could be useful in the bulk scanning of
foreign material for key phrases indicating items appearing to merit human attention. Its study has also
advanced the development of computer science - the usual
'fall-out' argument.

(7.3) IQ tests can be criticized, inter alia, as:

(a) culture-biassed, i.e. they assume familiarity with,
say, a Western European country's language, graphic
conventions and customs - which a computer system
would be unlikely to have;

(b) rating too highly the kind of intelligence, and
the concept of intelligence, that their designers
possess;

(c) undervaluing alogical, non-arithmetical aspects of
intelligence - though this might favour the machine system;

(d) treating initiative and creativity as independent
of intelligence, which, again, might favour the
computer in the earlier stages.

Machine	being more logical, less intuitive, would
intelligence:	find multiple answers to many of the ques
	ions and fail to select the one chosen to
	score. Also, for some time, machine in-
	telligence will tend to specialize, and
	thus not score well in tests covering a
	wide variety of problem situations.

(7.4)   The commonly quoted figure is 10^{10}, based on the anatom
cal work of Cajal and others around the beginning of
this century. For a large computer the number of logical elements – apart from the binary cells of its main
store – is about 10^5 to 10^6. The complexity of behaviour of a logical system increases much more rapidly
than in direct proportion to the number of cells in it.
Whence, our brains should be very much more subtle instruments than computers, even allowing for redundancy
of function; but in the simple tasks the computer's
great speed advantage allows it to out-perform us.

(7.5)   See par. 7.3.2

(7.6)   Initially, at least, creativity, initiative, purposeful
ness, the choice of goals, moral responsibility, aesthe
tic appreciation, sense of humour, emotional tone, etc.
etc.

(7.7)   By sensitivity analyses (see par. 7.1) providing a part
ial substitute for the experiments which economists are
not able to perform.

(7.8)   True of almost all our 'serious' (non-playful) activities, for the recognition of patterns underlies our per
ception of significance and meaning in speech and writing; and the detection of regularities and rhythms in
nature, art and society. 'Commonplace' rather than
'trivial', for if we were unable to detect patterns the
world would face us with a bewildering flux of apparently random phenomena.

(7.9)   Suppose – after Shannon – a typical chess game to com-
        prise 40 moves, with 10 alternatives at each stage.
        There are 10^{40} possibilities to evaluate. A fast com-
        puter executes 10^7 instructions/sec., hence, if (but
        improbably) it could evaluate 10^5 possible moves/sec.,
        then 10^{35} seconds would be needed, i.e. 3×10^{27} years.
        Even a computer 300 million times faster would require
        10^{19} years, i.e. about 1000 million times the postula-
        ted age of the universe.

(7.10) A computer-controlled machine tool could reproduce good
        copies of a specified piece of sculpture. It could al-
        so generate an indefinitely large number of shapes hav-
        ing random, or mathematically described, surfaces. The
        essence of the problem is to identify which, if any,
        among those shapes has artistic significance; and we
        neither know how to program the selection criteria, nor
        would we agree on what they should be.

(8.1)   Professions do preserve the privileges of their members,
        and have been known to surround their arts with a denser
        aura of mystique than is justified; but are there no
        useful functions? See par. 8.1

(8.2)   (a) *Strongly affected* because of high numerical and
             mathematical content: Accountancy, Engineering,
             Science, Defence services.

        (b) *Less affected* because largely non-numerical, with
             many qualitative judgements: Medicine, Law, Litera-
             ture, the Church.

(8.3)   See par. 8.3.2
        Certainly, 'real life' is a highly complex aggregate of
        phenomena, and simplification of it is always risky –
        whence, the less simplification the less danger, *provided*
        always that such simplification as we cannot avoid making
        has not removed the vital elements! Complication should

be soundly based, and not mere ad hoc elaboration to patch up a crumbling model. It can only carry us so far - the only *perfect* model of a ship is another identical ship.

(8.4) See par. 8.3.2

Precision: how many digits are used to express the quantity.

Accuracy: how near is it to the actual value.

Calculator precision: See par. 1.5

(8.5) See par. 8.1

Does computing have an intellectual base? require a disciplined study? need qualifications and tests of competence? guard an important part of our techno-culture? require the exercise of social responsibility' and a high degree of commercial ethics?

(8.6) See par. 8.1

Engineering at the professional level is not just a box of technical tricks. The selection of the appropriate tool for the particular circumstances, the assessing of the range of conditions that the design must meet, co-ping with unforeseeable situations, and a clear under-standing of the limitations of the design method, can all be important. The value of the professional engin-eer emerges just where the standard formulae fail - and this is where package programs would also lose their value.

(8.7) When writing a program everything has to be made comple-tely plain; nothing can be fudged by vague general state-ments, or left as an exercise to the computer. Moreover the analysis has to be made from a different viewpoint, and seeing the problem from this may reveal it in a new light.

(8.8)   See par. 8.2.3

Symptoms, as opposed to medical signs, are qualitative and highly subjective assessments made by untrained − and ill − people: they are therefore rather poor data for processing by a computer. Again, is it too simplistic to analyse in terms of objective 'diseases' waiting to be identified? Are there only sick patients?

(8.9)   See par. 8.2.4 on pre-flight trainers. A valuable aid in preparing for, or extending, road work; but not a complete substitute for it. The occasional lapses of other drivers could not be predicted, or reasonably programmed.

(8.10) As for St. Paul; see par. 8.2.7; it could be applied to the Bacon controversy.

(9.1)   See par. 9.1.1

Note that numerical analysis reduces advanced mathematics to simple arithmetical sequences.

(9.2)   No. The managing director should eschew detail, his function lies at the strategic level of management. See par. 9.1.3.

(9.3)   This extension is reasonable *provided* the enlarged situation is sufficiently well understood, and all necessary data can be acquired at the right times and with appropriate accuracy. The larger the area of control, the greater and more troublesome are the ramifications of misconceptions and errors; and the more susceptible is the whole to external disturbance − unless it is designed as a loosely-knit set of autonomous sub-systems. Uncontrolled factors include: industrial disputes, political pressures, international economic events, weather e.g. storms at sea, plant failures, etc.

(9.4)   (a) Machine tool control, with the computer interpreting a product specification into settings of tool speeds, depths and directions of cut; and correcting the operation continuously by feedback from instruments measuring the finished product.

(b) Management Information System, in which business operations are controlled and directed in terms of information about men, money, materials, production and markets. This information can never be complete, and prediction is never wholly accurate over the period between taking a decision and its taking effect on sales and earnings: hence, the control is partial.

(c) Economic and weather forecasting, even though increasingly elaborate models are being developed for each. Totally random - acybernetic - processes are hard to find, for there is almost always some residual bias; but electronic random number generators can produce uncontrolled and unpredictable results, e.g. the Post Office's Premium Bond Machine, ERNIE. For such as these, a computer's only role is in applying statistical tests to show that the results appear to be free from regularities.

(9.5) Both, they are complementary features of information systems. The database provides a common point of reference for all departments, and allows each to use the others' data.

(9.6) Where the separate users have a joint interest in:

(a) a common set of functions, e.g. LACES, see par. 9.1.4.

(b) a common set of data, as in a databank, e.g. stock exchange trading information, see par. 9.1.4.

(c) a common set of facilities, as in a multiaccess system for a university, or a commercial computer bureau.

Problems: privacy and protection from mutual interfer-

ence; security and reliability; equitable
costing and charging for actual use; economic provision of capacity to cope with demand peaks in a fluctuating load.

(9.7)   See par. 9.1.5

Operational, economic, or political (as opposed to managerial) reasons may indicate centralization, or its
reverse.

(9.8)   See par. 9.1.6;   also 9.1.3 and 9.1.5

(9.9)   (a)   it is usually easier to teach programming to the
scientist than for a lay programmer to achieve
sufficient understanding of the scientist's problems to make a useful contribution. Moreover,
programming efficiency is not always necessary,
e.g. for short, ephemeral programs, and where it
is necessary we can usually find a member of the
scientific establishment who has become hooked on
programming.

(b)   the length, complexity, and need for efficiency of
many commercial programs demands the use of professional programmers, and they have little difficulty
in comprehending the specifications of commercial
work.

(c)   generally as for science; but the need for efficiency is paramount, and there is no effective alternative to training control engineers thoroughly in
programming.

(9.10) See par. 9.2.4

(10.1) The traditional arguments turn on

(a)   reduced imports and possible exports,

(b)   vital component of productivity in manufacturing
and service industries, whose supply cannot be left
to the mercy of foreign competitors,

(c)   valuable pace-setter in electronics development,

(d)   essential part of the commercial, social and defence 'infra-structure' over which a nation must have sovereignty. The counter argument is: free enterprise, and no government interference.

Foreign ownership of nationally based companies leaves production at risk from commercial decisions taken in a foreign country; and national development know-how is applied to hone the competitive edge of the foreign product.

(10.2) Widely true: thus, the student demonstrator rarely wishes his protest to pass unreported; but would resent it being used at some future date to deny him a job. The dissatisfied customer, who refuses to pay, welcomes publicity; but resents being denied future credit as a bad payer.

(10.3) See par. 10.2

(a)   Personal records to be purged annually of all entries more than, say, 10 years old.

(b)   Personal records to be kept by an independent 'archival' authority which itself makes no use of them, and which controls all access to them.

(c)   Forbidden categories of data not to be recorded, e.g. political and religious affiliations, private reading lists (obtained from libraries or periodical circulation records), membership of societies.

(10.4) Politics reflects, more or less imperfectly, the desire of electors and their opinions on how best to achieve them. These desires and opinions rarely, if ever, rest on pure reason. Again, total rationality would require total information, but we have neither adequate theories nor the necessary data for many of the matters that concern governments.

(10.5) See par. 10.1

(10.6) See par. 10.2

Both need explicit regulation.

(10.7) See par. 10.3.1

Increases in productivity that are not matched by increases in output imply less working time, and thus more leisure, unless the freed time is absorbed by increased time spent on domestic chores or on travelling to work. This unsought, enforced, leisure will be unwelcome to those who lack the will or the means to fill it; and its yawning emptiness could give rise to some severe social problems – until we are all educated for leisure, as well as trained for work (not least for work that automation is about to make obsolete).

(10.8) (a)   Automation, productivity and unemployment.

(b)   Computer assisted planning as an aid (or hindrance) to economic growth.

(c)   Computer manufacture as a stimulus to the development of an advanced electronics industry.

(d)   Social consequences of introducing computer systems for those who work on them, or are affected by them, and also for society at large.

(e)   The tactical and strategic implications of the increased strike-power conferred on the handful of workers who program and operate computer systems.

(10.9) See par. 10.5

Populism is not the same as democracy.

(10.10) By unremitting attempts to explain in lay terms, but without condescension or infantile simplification, how the decisions taken derive from the facts of the case and the policies of the government. And, by resolutely refusing ever to blame 'the computer' for failures, or for unpopular actions. Generally, by avoiding the too-common denigration of the role of reason in human affairs – that is refusing to commit 'La trahison des clercs'.

Appendix 2 · Laces – a brief case history

ORIGIN

1. In 1966 a number of the international airlines formed a
    group of their cargo managers to study the ways in which
    a computer could be used to simplify and speed up the im-
    port procedures for airfreight at London's Heathrow air-
    port. The group met regularly over the next 18 months,
    considered how the office processes could be streamlined,
    and wrote a report of 114 pages which described in con-
    siderable detail a possible computer system, and made a
    very broad estimate of its cost. H.M. Customs had joined
    in the study, and the proposed system also covered its
    work of assessing duty and issuing clearances. This re-
    port constituted a statement of the users' requirement
    which was sufficiently detailed and comprehensive to show
    the feasibility of the proposal, and to serve as the Job
    Requirement Specification.

2. The airlines compete with each other in carrying cargo,
    and a substantial number of independent importing agents
    competes with them, and with each other, in providing coll-
    ecting and clearance services to the consignees: again,
    the Customs' interests differ from those of the agents and
    the airlines. However, all of them require data from the
    same files of cargo information, and their requirements
    could be met by a single, shared, real-time computer system
    providing 24-hours x 365-days a year service to 100 remote
    terminals in the airlines' offices and cargo sheds, plus
    another 50 terminals in H.M. Customs' offices and between

90 and 110 terminals to be shared by about 180 importing agents. All of these terminals would be located within the boundary of the airport.

DESIGN AND PROVISION

3. The users agreed that it would be preferable for some independent party to provide and operate the computer system on a commercial basis, and the Post Office's National Data Processing Service (NDPS) was eventually commissioned to do so, under the control of a project Steering Committee on which the users and NDPS were each represented. Over the period 1968 to 1971 NDPS carried out the tasks listed below.

(a) Determined and specified in detail the equipment required, sought and evaluated tenders, and bought: A twin computer system, special-purpose real-time software, and as remote terminals: 250 VDU's, and 70 character printers.

(b) Selected and acquired a site for the computer centre, designed and had erected an air-conditioned building with radar screening, regulated and protected power supplies, and telecommunication data links to the terminal sites in the users' offices.

(c) Assigned a team of systems analysts to design a computer system that the Steering Committee accepted would meet its requirements: the specification of this system in the degree of detail needed for its programming absorbed 212 man-years of effort, and the resulting 38,000 printed pages occupied several feet of shelving in large loose-leaf binders.

(d) Established programming teams to monitor the production of the special-purpose software by a subcontractor, and designed, specified, coded and tested the large suites of real-time and batch operational programs needed to meet the agreed systems specification: all of this absorbed 180 man-years.

(e) Designed and carried out acceptance tests on the hardware - including the building services, and on the software and the operational programs. Tests were required not only to check that the system was free from faults and errors, but also to determine that it would be able to carry the peak traffic load that was expected to develop during its 9-year economic life. Special test programs were written, and masses of test data were prepared and analysed - 10,000 individual tests involving a total of 100,000 test inputs were made; the whole process occupied about 22 man-years of work in the preparation of test data, and 11 man-years for the testing and analysis over a period of 4 weeks! A large group of students on vacation operated the remote terminals in order to generate a saturation load of randomly-timed traffic having the correct mix of input data and interrogations, and the system's response was carefully checked for accuracy and speed as the load was built up.

(f) Recruited and trained an operating staff of 35 to man the computer around the clock - and around the calendar too.

(g) Prepared operating manuals, and ran training course for 1500 members of the users' staffs who would be using the remote terminals.

(h) Took over the maintenance of the real-time software and of the operational programs; this work provides a full-time load for 19 programmers.

4. The computer hardware alone cost about £3 millions; and
the systems, software and programming costs amounted to
about another £2½ millions. At its peak, the preparatory
work engaged a team of 180 men and women.

OPERATION

5. The total-system tests revealed about 1000 program and
software errors remaining after the separate preliminary
tests, but these were corrected within 6 weeks and the
first users were connected to the system in the middle of
1971, within 5 weeks of the ready-for-service date which
had been quoted by NDPS three years previously. The remaining users were connected to the system over the next
few months according to an agreed schedule, and LACES became fully operational. In 1975, after four years of
operation, the system was serving 206 remote VDU's and
62 remote character printers.

6. The airlines feed in data from waybills sent ahead from
the departure airport, which show what items have been
loaded on a particular aircraft bound for Heathrow. On
arrival, the airline staff record what has actually been
unloaded, and where each item has been placed in their
cargo sheds; and their charges are calculated. The importing agents use the computer terminal to make customs
declarations on behalf of their clients. H.M. Customs
decide which parcels to open for physical examination,
and command the computer to print a note of these on the
terminal nearest to where they are being stored in the
cargo sheds, so that the warehouseman can get them out in
readiness. The customs officer uses a shed terminal to
make his inspection report. The computer calculates the
customs duties, and records data for the government's
trade statistics.

7. The agents can interrogate the computer at any time to check the 'status' of a particular parcel – has it left the distant airport? arrived at Heathrow? been assessed by Customs? etc. Before a parcel can be collected, the airline charges and the customs duties have to be paid; and it will not be released from the cargo shed until the computer has notified the warehouseman that this has been done. The computer's common database provides a fast and effective communication system for coordinating the work of the airlines, the agents and H.M. Customs. As one illustration of this, a few months after LACES was fully operational it was noticed that the number of telephone calls being made at the airport had fallen by 100,000 a month; they had been replaced by approximately 1,000,000 calls a month to the computer. Each authorized user has an individual plastic card which is magnetically coded, and which he has to insert into his terminal in order to operate; the card identifies him as a legitimate user of that particular terminal and for specific purposes only. In this way the users, although competing, can operate without mutual interference, and when a card is lost it can be instantly disabled by the central operator altering its expiry date to yesterday.

8. The LACES computer room is very large and filled with equipment, but it has a strangely quiet air, for real-time operation provides little work for the central operators – except when things go wrong! At any moment the computer handling requests from some 200 terminals, which have to dealt with by a wide variety of programs, called up as necessary according to the type of request. Up to 500 enquiries/minute can be handled, and the response to a straight forward request is completed within 2 seconds. No one knows precisely what the computer is doing at any instant

and no one needs to know. The files are kept on exchange-able magnetic disks and the data in them are ephemeral, for once a parcel has been collected its data can be de-leted. Batch processing programs weed the files, and take periodic copies (dumps) of them on magnetic tapes for the purpose of answering any delayed queries that may arise.

RESULTS

9. The most important result has been an improved service to the public by reducing delays in clearing air cargo through Heathrow; the average parcel is now delivered within two days of landing, as compared with $4\frac{1}{2}$ days under the previous system. This speed-up has yielded savings in the offices concerned; pressure on space in the cargo sheds has been reduced — allowing their enlargement to be postponed; the same number of Customs staff has been able to cope with a growing traffic; and the work of the im-porting agents has changed from chasing the airlines to deliver, to chasing their clients to collect.

10. At a later stage LACES will be linked directly to similar systems in other countries, when these have been installed, and work has already begun on extending the scope of the system to serve terminals remote from the airport, to serve other British airports, and to cover exports also.

11. The success of the scheme was largely due to the fact that the initial statement of requirements was prepared extre-mely thoroughly by users who knew exactly what they wanted to do, and who had themselves had considerable experience of data processing, and also to the fact that it was im-plemented by an organization with much previous experience of designing and operating very large commercial computer systems. In particular, the systems analysis and design were completed in great detail, and fully documented and agreed by the users, before any programs were written.

Index